GETTING THERE FROM HERE

Also by Elizabeth Goldsmith:

God Can Be Trusted
Your Guide to Guidance (*with Martin Goldsmith*)

GETTING THERE FROM HERE

How to Find Your Place in God's Global Picture

ELIZABETH GOLDSMITH

M
publishing
CARLISLE, UK

© Elizabeth Goldsmith 1986, 1995

First published 1986 by Marc Europe
in association with STL Books and the Evangelical Missionary
Alliance

This revised edition 1995 by OM Publishing

01 00 99 98 97 96 95   7 6 5 4 3 2 1

OM Publishing is an imprint of Send the Light Ltd.,
P.O. Box 300, Carlisle, Cumbria CA3 0QS, U.K.

Unless otherwise stated, Scripture quotations
in this publication are from the Holy Bible,
New International Version.
Copyright © 1973, 1978, 1984 by International Bible Society.
Published by Zondervan and Hodder & Stoughton.

British Library Cataloguing in Publication Data

Goldsmith, Elizabeth
    Getting There from Here: How to Find Your
    Place in God's Global Picture. – 2Rev.ed
    I. Title
    266

    ISBN 1–85078–230–x

Typeset by Photoprint, Torquay, Devon
and Printed in the U.K. by Cox and Wyman Ltd., Reading

Contents

To Martin,
without whose ideas, wealth of experience
and never-failing encouragement
(or was it bullying?),
this book would never have been written.

Introduction

We are living in days of unprecedented opportunity for Christian mission. World-shattering events have taken place in recent years which will go down in history books as key dates. The power of the former U.S.S.R. has crumbled, so that many countries previously under its domination are now wide open for the gospel of Jesus Christ. Marxism, Christianity's most implacable persecutor this century, has revealed its inherent poverty, spiritually and materially, leaving a vacuum that something must fill. Its rapid collapse, accompanied by relatively little violence, must surely have been in answer to the prayers of God's people.

Yet in China her leaders still cling tenaciously to their outdated ideology while giving free reign to blatant materialism. So the church in China now faces the additional threat posed by mammon, alongside her many years of restriction and persecution. She needs our help and prayers as never before.

The constantly changing political and economic situations in our day present an on-going challenge. The memory of recession in western countries causes unrest and uncertainty which can only find its answers in the Christian faith. And we ask ourselves what developments in the wealth of the Pacific Rim Nations and the power of the European Union mean for the Christian church and mission.

Many of the major world religions are posing a growing threat to Christianity. Islam has gained in power and influence since the oil boom of the 1960s. Their new-found confidence expresses itself in some Islamic states in fundamentalism seeking to gain power. And this is violently

1

anti-Christian. We need to stand with God's people in these lands, and extend his kingdom even in the face of such opposition. Courage must go hand in hand with wisdom. Eastern religions sound increasingly attractive to young westerners brought up in frenetic activism and on a diet that 'science holds all the answers'. The church of God must wake up to what is happening in traditionally 'Christian' countries, and mobilise against superstition and secularism.

Meanwhile the horrendous economic gap between the priviledged nations and those less fortunate lays on us a burden of responsibility as we worship the God of love who created all mankind. While at the same time, the uprooting of peoples from areas stricken by poverty, famine or war has deepened their need. Others who have sought refuge in the west have now become far more accessible to the ordinary church member. The 'mission field' has come to our doorstep.

Although the church of Jesus Christ has grown by unprecedented numbers in the last century there still remain some areas with little or no Christian witness and with no Scriptures in their own language. Yet there is a hunger and openness among many people, and a searching for a spiritual dimension to life.

In the light of these world situations I want in this book to show clearly what are the needs and opportunities facing the church today, what kind of person is needed for the missionary task, and what are the various routes open to us in 'Getting There from Here'. I shall attempt to show that the concept of world-wide mission runs like a thread throughout the whole Bible. And I hope to shed light on some very practical questions such as: how can I know God's will for my life? How should I prepare? And how might I be supported?

As we prayerfully view the world today we see a great harvest ready to be gathered in. We who long to know the name of our Lord and Saviour uplifted as it deserves to be must buy up the opportunities of the present moment.

1
What are the Needs Today?

Church-based missionary work
The key to the evangelisation of the world lies in the mobilisation of the local churches. They are familiar with the local language and customs. They can identify with the world-view of their neighbours, and convey the Christian message relevantly.

All expatriates sound and feel foreign until they have been in a country many years. And even then they may not understand the local situation fully. But they can be invaluable in mobilising local Christians by example and by teaching. And energy channeled in this way can yield a fruitful harvest.

The local church may be comparatively insignificant or even fairly large; but as it catches the vision for what can be done, the resulting growth will be fully appropriate and indigenous. Today there are very few areas in the world without a Christian presence somewhere in the vicinity. So our rightful desire to 'reach the unreached' in pioneer evangelism may often be best achieved by working in, under and through national churches.

My husband and I worked for some years in the Karo Batak churches of North Sumatra. At that time between them they had a membership of some 20,000 mainly scattered across a mountainous plateau 4–5,000 feet high. The growth of these churches had been fairly slow, although the central church in Kabanjahe sometimes had a congregation of nearly 1,000. Under God's grace we were priviledged to see the beginnings of a vast turning to Christ. But when we returned to the U.K. for our first home leave we remember being asked:

'But if the churches overseas are so large and growing so quickly, why do we have to send missionaries there at all?'

The baffled student who flung this question at my husband was grappling with a problem. Of course, not all churches overseas are large and fast growing, and we shall come to these others in a moment. But first, in order to understand my husband's answer, pause a moment to picture the size of the congregation of your own church. Let us say, for the sake of argument, that you have 100 members. In our first two years among the Karo Bataks of Indonesia, the membership of our churches grew by 25 per cent. If the same had happened in your church, your 100 members would now have become 125. That is easy enough; you can disciple an extra 25 Christians and integrate them quite easily into your church's life. But in the following three or four years, the Karo church membership trebled. On the example of your own church you would now suddenly have 375 people, and your resources would be stretched to the limit. How could you teach them properly? There would now be far more young Christians than mature ones. Who would counsel them in their problems and pastor them as they began to apply Christian morals to their daily lives?

Over the next few years the numbers of Karo Christians grew steadily, so that when we visited them 20 years later the membership had increased by seven times! Long before this you would have sent an SOS to a nearby church: 'Please come and help us. We can't cope with all our new Christians!' But they might have replied, 'We're swamped ourselves! We too are desperately short of workers'. Added to this the Karos would have said, 'We need more Bible study aids. We have no suitable books for our Christians. There is no one to train our Sunday School teachers. And how can our elders teach the baptismal candidates when they know so little themselves?'

With the staggering growth of your church, you might even be driven to looking further afield for help. And if a Christian from another part of the world offered to come, one who knew your country and its language and customs well, and who had had thorough training in how to build up a lay ministry, how thankfully you might appoint them onto your team of church elders!

The above situation was the position in which many missionaries found themselves in Indonesia when we worked there. Some were training lay leaders to care for home groups. Some gave elders further teaching in Christian doctrine and how it applies to everyday life. Many preached in the mushrooming churches where, on average, each ordained minister cared for twelve congregations. Some had specialised skills which they gave to preparation of nation-wide Sunday School material, or of Religious Education teaching material throughout the schools of Indonesia. Some concentrated on producing Christian literature, encouraging and aiding the national Christian publishing body in the translation of many books including the massive IVP *New Bible Commentary*. At the same time they aimed to stimulate national authors to write. Others pioneered distribution channels so that the books were more readily available. Some lectured in the universities advising and counselling the students, and helping with the setting up of Christian Unions.

Fast growing churches are a prime example of places where skilled missionary personnel might be greatly appreciated. Pouring their expertise into the national church, by God's grace they can revive churches with little vision, bring in fresh ideas from overseas, and stimulate local missionary vision. Today these same Karo Batak churches have grown to a quarter of a million and are now sending their own missionaries to neighbouring races and further afield. Recently my husband met two of them working among Muslims in the Philippines.

Korea today has huge, well-taught churches. Most of these are reformed Presbyterian, but there are also some Methodist and Pentecostal ones. Some years ago, when one major missionary society surveyed the country to see what the needs of the churches might be, its representatives came back with two formulated goals: firstly, to encourage personal Bible study among Korean Christians to whom it was a new discipline, and secondly, to instil in them a missionary vision which would tap the potential of their enormous churches and benefit the whole world. Today, as well as more individual Bible study being stressed, there is a great upsurge of interest in missionary work throughout the country. One international mission leader said there were so many Koreans offering themselves for overseas service, there could easily be 1,000 candidates from Korea each year. What is needed there now is missionary training institutes which understand the reality of church-related and cross-cultural mission. They need help in how to prepare their large number of workers for mission, especially how to work in humility and with a 'servant spirit' under local leadership.

Every church, from the more recently founded to the old-established ones, has its strengths and weaknesses. We all have things we are good at, and we all have areas where we would benefit from some help. Although it is a generalisation, it would be true to say the Lutheran church in Norway has a long history of theological expertise but would be much refreshed by a breath of new life such as swept through East Africa in the revival. Many British churches have skills in pastoral care and biblical exposition and have access to a dazzling variety of books with teaching on almost every subject one can think of. Yet many of these very churches are weak on evangelism. But I once watched a Chilean evangelist at work for three months in a large Anglican church and saw how his spirituality and methods revolutionised their attempts at making Christ known. All who have had the privilege to sit at the feet of great men of God like Festo Kivengere of Uganda and Chandapilla of India have been greatly enriched in their own spiritual lives. And God is raising up evangelists like Luis Palau who are gifted in bringing the good news of Jesus Christ right across cultural boundaries.

'Where then is the mission field?' a new American recruit was heard to ask on landing in Hong Kong and visiting a large mission-minded church on his first Sunday. The answer is, 'The field is the world'. (Matthew 13:38) We *all* have need of the expertise which others can give. We *all* have responsibility to share our own skills with others.

Those who feel that the need at home is so great ask, 'How can we possibly share our workers with churches overseas? We can't spare them.' But was this how the church in Antioch responded to the Holy Spirit's directive to extract Paul and Barnabas from their leadership team and move them on somewhere else? Maybe we presume it was easy for those early Christians, but let us stop and think how Paul's dynamic leadership and Barnabas' gift of encouragement would have been sadly missed. The scriptural basis of giving is not to give what we can easily spare, but to give sacrificially, where it hurts (II Samuel 24:24; II Corinthians 8:2–5). It is to those who have given far more than they can spare that the promise comes: 'God is able to make all grace abound to you, so that in all things at all times, having all that you need, you will abound in every good work.' (II Corinthians 9:8) If the Lord of the harvest is asking our church to give some of its best workers to go overseas, can we argue with him? Surely he knows best. If missionaries had not brought the Gospel to Europe and the shores of America, where would we be today?

Needs for evangelism

Yet there are also situations where an expatriate is needed to pioneer evangelism. For instance, in some countries the churches may be strong but they have so far neglected whole sections of the population. It may take a 'foreigner' to highlight the situation and pioneer ways of overcoming the lack. The rapidly expanding Pentecostal churches of Chile and Argentina are doing an excellent job reaching the lower classes and shanty-town dwellers. Their evident spirituality and the warmth of their love have attracted many hundreds of thousands of people to Christ. One church my husband visited had to limit members of its congregation to one visit to the central church every five weeks. The church could *only* hold 16,000 people, and the total membership was 80,000! But they were making no impact whatsoever on the middle and upper classes. It took the arrival of Anglican missionaries to make an impact there. These expatriate workers came from middle class backgrounds, and this helped them to relate easily with the better-off families.

My husband was once on a plane flying between two South American countries and found himself sitting next to a refined, beautifully coiffeured business woman. She was interested to know what brought this Englishman to her country. He replied that he was a missionary. She took that in her stride as she was used to the many Catholic missionary orders. But when he mentioned he was Protestant she studied him carefully and exclaimed, 'Oh how interesting! I've never met one of those before!' When he laughingly told us the story he added, 'I felt like a three-humped camel in a zoo!'. But the experience did underline the paucity of evangelical impact among upper-class South Americans.

There are parts of the world where churches exist but dare not, or are unwilling to cross cultural barriers in evangelism. In Jordan the traditionally 'Christian' communities are free to work actively among their own folk, but if the government got wind of their engaging in Muslim evangelism they would face real problems. This is where 'outsiders' have a place, in wise, low-key evangelism to Muslims. Not being directly linked with local churches they are not implicating them in their work. The example of their witness may encourage national Christians to engage in wise evangelism, even if it leads to suffering.

Other churches find it difficult to reach out to their neighbours because of big differences in culture and language. For instance, the churches in Bangladesh are almost all filled with people of Hindu origin. They use Hindu terminology for words like God, worship, sin, and follow Hindu culture in their structure and forms of worship. But the large majority of people in Bangladesh are Muslim, and when they are converted they find it difficult to become integrated into Hindu-type churches. Missionaries have therefore pioneered an attempt to set up churches which will cater expressly for Muslim converts. Their expressions of worship are more in line with their Muslim upbringing, and Arabic terms are chosen for key concepts. This would have been a difficult exercise for a local church, but missionaries from outside found it possible. And now Bangladeshi Muslim converts have caught the vision of forming contextual Muslim-background groups.

There are many countries today where much evangelism has been taking place, yet untouched racial groups or segments of society still remain. These isolated pockets of people (sometimes forming very large groups) will remain ignorant of the Gospel until someone catches a vision for going there. For instance, Kerala is the most Christianised state in India, with a long tradition dating right back to the founding of the old Mar Thoma church. Yet almost all the Christians are to be found in the very high or very low castes. The middle castes have few Christians.

A recent survey in Singapore showed over one-third of all graduates to be converted evangelical Christians. But the large majority of Christians are Chinese, and relatively little work is being done among Muslim Malays.

Coming nearer home, how many Christians are there on the factory floor, in coal mines or steel works? Very few indeed! Or can we find many in the heavy industries in the West German Ruhr district? Perhaps we need workers from other countries to show us how to reach artisan areas in our own industrial working class.

Apart from these untouched groups of people, there are still countries in the world where the Christian population is abysmally small. How can we remain complacent at the thought that nearly 2,000 years have elapsed since Jesus Christ won our salvation at such terrible cost, and there are still hundreds of thousands of people who have not heard? Looking through the pages of a *National Geographic* magazine, I saw photos of the staggering crush of pilgrims around the Ka'abah in Mecca. Forcibly it was brought home to me that there are large areas of North Africa and the Arabian peninsula where so far we of the world-wide church have largely failed to make an impact.

There are parts of Japan where one can still drive hour after hour without passing a Christian church. Large areas in Burma and Bhutan have no Christian witness whatsoever. Many villages in India have never been reached for Christ. Huge sections of Bangladesh and Pakistan do not know Christ. Turkey, which used to have a sizeable Christian population, now has very few. Countries like Kazakhstan and Uzbekistan have considerable Russian churches but relatively few Christians from among the indigenous peoples. And the doors are wide open now to these former Communist areas, whose churches are unaccustomed to open evangelism. Of course, some countries do not allow missionaries as such, but there are other ways of gaining entry, such as using professional skills to obtain work. And even some of the Communist countries are beginning to open up to trade and the professions. For instance, after over 40 years of closed doors to foreigners, China is now allowing outsiders to come in for specialist professional work and business investment. With wise handling, this is opening up immense opportunities for the world-wide church once more to encourage Chinese Christians.

Next to the outstanding needs of the Islamic world and countries influenced by Marxism, southern Europe presents us with a challenge. The evangelical churches in these strongly Roman Catholic countries are desperately small and in need of outside help in their evangelistic task.

The church of Jesus Christ must wake up to the alarming fact of the unevangelised areas of the world. Her Master challenges: 'Lift up your eyes, and look on the fields!' The word 'look' in the original Greek does not mean 'give a cursory glance'. It implies 'gaze at, take in the situation, study'. These are the needs of the world. We as Christians must allow them to sink into our consciousness and affect us radically.

Para-church activities

An important aspect of pursuing our basic target of world evangelisation and the building up of the church of Jesus Christ, both at home and abroad, is what might be termed 'para-church' activities. This carries the idea of working alongside the church, 'para' coming from Greek and meaning 'alongside'. Today there is a wide variety of opportunities for serving Jesus Christ in this sort of work all around the world.

The work of the Universities and Colleges Christian Fellowship and its international body, the International Fellowship of Evangelical Students, has been outstanding in bringing to Christ men and women who have taken up positions of leadership in all walks of life. Large numbers of gifted young men and women have been trained in Bible knowledge and the spiritual disciplines, making an incalculable impact on the church worldwide. Other groups like Campus Crusade for Christ and Navigators have joined this ministry and are playing their part in challenging young people all around the world to dedicate themselves fully to living for Christ. They would all welcome more trained workers for this strategic task.

Groups who work in schools, like Youth for Christ and Scripture Union, are playing a vital role. Other people have had a vision for setting up Christian Unions in hospitals among the medical workers, or in offices, shops and factories. Their unique position right on location enables them to reach people who would not normally come to church, giving them a strategic part to play.

There is huge scope in the field of communications for Christians to use their skills to make Christ known. For years Christian radio stations have beamed the message of the Bible into countries of every political and religious persuasion. Television programmes and more recently, computer networking are also being used. These require men and women with all sorts of expertise. Some are needed to set up and maintain the equipment, others to produce the programmes, people who are actors, script writers, photographers and directors. A well-known preacher may reach a few thousand people a year, but those involved in mass media have audiences in hundreds of thousands.

All that is involved in Bible translation, printing and distribution provides immense scope for dedicated Christians to minister to people in other countries. The work of the Wycliffe Bible Translators has drawn the attention of the worldwide church to the many races who as yet do not possess the Scriptures in their own tongue. People with linguistic skills, stickability and sensitivity to other cultures are needed to undertake translation work. Alongside these, others with literacy ability can work to teach reading skills and to produce simple primers.

Men and women with vision are setting up Christian publishing agencies all over the world, producing complete Bibles and portions of Scripture for sale, but more are needed. The wealth of Christian books that we feast upon in the West needs to be shared with other countries. The most suitable ones should be translated into other languages, and national writers should be trained to write relevantly for their own people. A network of distribution centres needs to be set up at the same time, making this literature as widely available as possible.

Do you have skills as a printer? Could you write lively and interesting Sunday School teaching aids? Could you help produce study manuals for theological students who are training at home under the supervision of a tutor? Have you worked on the editorial staff of a magazine, or do you have experience with layout and design? Have you gifts as a salesman which could be channeled into opening up a better distribution network for Christian books in a country overseas? The variety of gifts which can be used in the evangelisation of the world is immense. There are openings today as never before.

A warning

One caution, however, must be sounded concerning para-church activities. Are they ends in themselves? Or do they have the goal of building up the *church* in that country? We all fall so easily into the trap of building up *my own* work. The human heart can be so fickle, deceiving itself that it is engrossed in the Lord's business but gradually being deflected into erecting its own little kingdom. We might not admit it, but the success of 'our work' can surreptiously take over and become our prime goal.

The goal of our Lord was to build his Church, not a plethora of little independent ministries. 'I will build my church,' he announced the moment the disciples had grasped who he was (Matthew 16:16–18). Once they realised that he was the promised Messiah, the very Son of God, he began to unfold for them his plans for the future. His purpose was to build his Church, a body of people called out from the world to form a unique new society, 'a chosen race, a royal priesthood, a holy nation, God's own people', straddling all human boundaries of race and status and becoming the one, unique church of God worldwide.

It was 'to the church', not to separate establishments, that the Lord daily added those who were being saved (Acts 2:47). It was 'against the church' that persecution arose (Acts 8:1). In the New Testament the Church is thought of as the one new fellowship spreading out steadily and courageously through the world. The local gatherings of Christians are called 'the church in' a certain place, (see Revelation 2 and 3), with the idea that individual 'churches' are the local manifestation of the one central reality. And this reality, the Church of God universal, is called 'the body of Christ'. Jesus has set himself the task of building up the Church. Other ministries are useful, but his central purpose is to sanctify the *Church* in order 'that he might present the church to himself in splendour without spot or wrinkle or any such thing' (Ephesians 5:26,27). And 'the plan of the mystery hidden for ages in God' was 'that through the *church* the manifold wisdom of God might now be made known to the principalities and powers in the heavenly places' (Ephesians 3:9,10).

We need to ask ourselves, therefore, if this 'para-church' activity is building up the Church of Christ, or merely building itself. Is the activity of the various institutions and organisations geared to their own growth, or to the growth of the Church? Are the people who are involved in it so busy that they have no time for the Church? Or are its aims such that the Church is enriched, encouraged and strengthened?

Social ministries

The Bible teaches us that every man, woman and child on earth is made in the image of God. This does not just mean that our spiritual side is made in God's image, but that the whole person has been formed in God's likeness. Some

14

people have rightly criticised a past emphasis on 'winning souls for Christ', as if the church were only concerned with the spiritual dimension. We must not mentally separate soul from body. Jesus loved whole people, not just that part of them which had a capacity for relationship with his heavenly Father. He noticed when the crowds were hungry and fed them. He healed their bodies when they came to him for help. He taught those who were longing for truth, as seen, for instance, in Luke 10:39. He was aware of the emotional shock which the news of John the Baptist's death brought (Matthew 14:12,13), and lovingly took his disciples off to a quiet place, giving them space to recover.

Our task as ambassadors for Christ is therefore a 'holistic' mission, where we are aware of the total needs of each person we minister to. We cannot expect someone who is dying of hunger to listen to the good news of life in Christ. We must first feed them, caring for their physical needs before we have a right to speak. Indeed our very actions in themselves will be speaking, telling people they are of value, their welfare is important, they are worthy objects of love. And we shall have gained the right to say, 'We love you because the almighty God who made you loves you. He has sent us to you to tell you about his love.'

One of the current debates in mission today is, 'Which has priority, evangelism or social action?' I believe we should see the two together as constituent parts of mission. They form two sides of the same coin. Where there is physical need, evangelism must go hand in hand with relieving that need. Where social concern is being expressed in practical ways, there should also be a verbal expression of why we are acting in this way, an explanation of the love of Christ which motivates us (II Corinthians 5:14,15).

Do we need to remind each other of the desperate needs of two-thirds of the world? Our television news forces it in front of our gaze every week. Our newspapers are spattered with accounts of floods in this country, drought in that. World economic structures apparently inexorably prise wider and wider the gap between the 'haves' and the 'have-nots'. Desperate poverty, insecurity and sickness run rampant through nation after nation. Can we sit idly by? Can we who have light in our homes at the touch of a switch, fresh, clean water at the turn of a tap, shrug our shoulders at the needs of others?

Is God calling you to train as a doctor or nurse to meet some of these needs? Where are the engineers with skills to bore water-holes, or ability to build roads so that supplies can be brought? Who is training as an agriculturalist or nutritionist to help tackle the world's food problems? Who has skills of administration to supervise the distribution of aid which has been given and to ensure its speedy, safe delivery to the places which need it most?

For many years missions have played, and still do play, a major role in all these areas of social action. And they are in a good position to do so, since their team of workers is there at grass-roots level. Unlike many other aid schemes they have personnel who are already familiar with the country, who know its language and customs and social structures. They have a clearer view of the real needs and how best to meet them. Some time ago my husband stayed with a banking consultant in Denmark. He was describing the third world aid programme set up by his own country, which had so often run into unforeseen snags. Much of the aid was leading to long-term dependency on the part of the recipients. Much was given in inappropriate forms: buildings which could not be maintained, vehicles which could not stand up to the local conditions or which no one knew how to repair. My husband was reminded of five tractors which had been donated by some well-wishing group to the Karo Bataks in North Sumatra, and how within a year they were all out of action because of misuse and lack of spare parts. He urged his Danish host to do all he could to channel the aid through local missionaries who would be able to give the crucial advice needed, an approach largely taken, for instance, by the Swedish government.

Getting There From Here

Support teams

'Now that I have been appointed onto the home staff,' a fellow missionary ruefully commented to me, 'the number of people wishing to take my prayer letters has fallen drastically.' His new job was just as demanding as his previous one, and needed considerable skill to handle, but there seemed an unspoken attitude, 'missionary work is done *out there*, not here at home.'

Another missionary I spoke to was having trouble raising his support. 'Who's really interested in the back-room boys?' he asked. 'My days are largely taken up with shopping lists for people up-country, with trailing from office to office about someone's exit or re-entry visa, or escorting missionary children in transit between home and school.' Yet his work was every bit as necessary as that of those who got all the lime-light. I wondered if his home church needed educating as to the real meaning of being a missionary.

As with any big organisation, there is a large number of back-up jobs needing to be done in missionary work. Finance needs to be efficiently handled. Buildings must be erected and kept in repair. Children of missionaries need to be educated, and cared for in their leisure hours if they are far from home. I heard of a couple in their fifties going to an Asian country for the first time to run the Mission Home in the capital city. A girl with editorial experience joined the home staff to re-vitalise the monthly magazine. A business director who had retired early spent six months looking into the administration of a mission and giving it an overhaul.

There are any amount of jobs to be done in the extention of the Church of Jesus Christ throughout the world. The needs are enormous and the opportunities immense. God can use both men and women, singles and marrieds, young and old. In many countries, relating across the sexes is not acceptable, so we need both men and women to reach the whole of society. People of quality and leadership ability can fill a wide variety of roles in mission. A foreign woman missionary may not threaten national leaders as much as a man; and

18

women fill many strategic places in theological and Bible teaching and church work, as well as in their own professions. Single people are often free from family distractions to give themselves wholly to the Lord's work, while marrieds can model Christian patterns for family life. The enthusiasm, zeal and motivation of younger workers can contribute a great deal, while older people add maturity and wisdom born out of experience. The latter may also be able to offer skilled expertise in business or some profession. By taking semi- or early retirement they can contribute markedly to the extension of God's kingdom. There is increasing scope today for this to happen.

Never before has the Church had so many tools at her command. Never before has communication been possible to so many people at one time. Never has travel been so fast, so easy and so efficient. Why do we hesitate to grasp the opportunities today? Why are we holding back from giving our all in the service of our Lord whose parting words were, 'Go into all the world and make disciples of all peoples' (Matthew 28:19)?

Questions for discussion

1. Some Christians say that evangelism has priority over social concern. Do you agree?
2. Should all Christian ministry be church-based?
3. What advantages or difficulties might you experience when working as an expatriate under national church leadership?
4. Having read about world-wide needs, where do you feel that you might fit in?

2

What Kind of Person is Needed?

If we had been able to ask the apostle Paul what kind of people he chose as his fellow missionaries, I wonder what his answer would have been. As we look at Paul himself we see an outstanding personality with an acute mind. He had been trained at one of the top schools of learning under a famous rabbi. He showed tremendous dedication to his task coupled with a clear-sighted strategy. For him, spiritual goals and values were of pre-eminent importance, so that his one aim in life was to know Christ and to do his will.

As we glimpse the many-faceted, brilliant character of Paul through the pages of the New Testament, we could be tempted to discouragement. Few of us would dare stand shoulder to shoulder with Paul in an evaluation of even one aspect of our lives. The whole spectrum of Paul's outstanding personality could fill us with dismay. As we look at him, the thought might easily arise, 'I could never qualify to serve God.'

Weakness
But there are aspects of Paul's life and writings which some today overlook. We live in a day when signs and wonders are

being brought into prominence. And Paul too saw the reality of God's power to heal and to defeat demonic powers. Yet woven into Paul's experience we see another emphasis. He writes:

> God chose the foolish things of the world to shame the wise. God chose the weak things of the world to shame the strong. He chose the lowly things of this world, and the despised things, and the things that are not — to nullify the things that are, so that no one may boast before him.
>
> 1 Corinthians 1:27–29

How did Paul come to write this way? What did this gifted man know of being weak or foolish or lowly? I would suggest these were lessons which God himself taught Paul through the fires of experience. In II Corinthians we are allowed the priceless privilege of looking at some of the traumas through which he has passed. 'We were under great pressure', he writes, 'far beyond our ability to endure, so that we despaired even of life . . . But this happened that we might not rely on ourselves but on God, who raises the dead.' (1:8,9). Several times in this letter he writes of the 'distress and anguish' he has suffered (2:4), he shares feelings of being crushed and perplexed (4:8–12), and he lists the terrible suffering he has experienced (6:4–10; 7:5 and others).

As one reads these words with sensitivity and understanding, a picture emerges of a man who has suffered deeply. We see a man who again and again was brought to the end of his own resources and who, in spite of his gifts, saw himself as intrinsically weak. He thus was able to admit gladly, 'We have this treasure in jars of clay to show that this all-surpassing power is from God and not from us' (4:7).

Paul is here making us aware of one of the paradoxes of the Christian life, which is that when we are weak, we are strong (c.f. II Corinthians 12:7–10). This whole letter would make a tremendously worthwhile study for anyone considering missionary work of any form. It underlines the fact that though we should attempt to develop to the full any gifts God has given us, ultimately in God's sight we are all weak. If we achieve anything, it is not our ability which has accomplished it, it is Christ's. As Jesus said, 'Apart from me you can do nothing' (John 15:5).

I am reminded of a letter I received recently from a young man who has spent the last 18 months waiting. He is longing to serve God in the South Sea islands, but for various reasons no decision has been made yet to accept him for service. This has been a painful time for him, revealing areas of need in his own personality and enabling him to begin to appropriate the healing which God is offering him. The experience will leave an indelible mark on his life, as he has faced up to his weakness as perhaps never before. And yet he has learnt to find his sufficiency in God. He finished his letter with, 'It's by *his grace and his mercy* that all this has happened, so I think the future is going to be exciting.' I, too, feel that will be so, since he has seen the reality of his weakness and the reality of God's grace.

Hudson Taylor was reckoned to be an outstanding missionary of the last century. He was one of the earliest pioneers of 'faith missions' and at one time had over 1,000 missionaries working with him in inland China. He was far ahead of his time in many of his practices, advocating identification with the local people in lifestyle, dress, and thorough grasp of the language.

Once when he was in a church speaking about the work of his mission someone came up to him afterwards and said, 'How amazing it must be to think that God has done all that through you!' He surveyed her quietly for a moment and then replied, 'Madam, I believe God was looking for someone weak enough and humble enough for him to be able to use. And he found me.'

Humility
An attitude of pride, even if unconscious, will seriously hinder our ministry to others. Those who are called of God

into cross-cultural mission need to be particularly aware of this. We may find ourselves in situations where people are what we might term 'unduly touchy' about their nationalism. Any implied superiority on our part, however unintentional, may meet with a stormy reception. We need to remember that ex-colonial countries had to submit for generations to indignity and injustice. They were often forced to be second-class citizens in their own country; and now that they hold the power, it is only human nature to let others feel it.

When we lived in Indonesia and had to go to a Government office for any matter, we had quietly to take a seat and wait until we were called. Other people who arrived long after us were likely to be served first; but it would have been quite out of place to have expostulated, 'But it's our turn next!' The clerk knew he was keeping us waiting, but he also knew that as a young man he had been kept waiting many, many times by some foreign official who claimed to have power in his country.

Living in another country quickly exposes in our hearts areas of pride we never knew were there. 'You can't cook cabbage like that, I've always done it this way!' a new missionary exclaimed. 'There is a much better way of cleaning windows than that,' another remonstrated. 'The best way to do evangelism is to organise large rallies,' someone else insisted, and embarked on a long description of how they evangelised back home. But different situations may call for different techniques, and for many issues there is no firm 'right' or 'wrong' way; there is just the method we have always seen and a multitude of other methods which our unimaginative minds have not pictured yet.

A spirit of humility needs to be cultivated so that we are ready and willing to learn from others. There may be a host of valid reasons why our long-cherished methods are not suitable in the new situation.

A pastor from northern Nigeria brought out a related point when my husband interviewed him. 'What would you look for in a new missionary to your country?' Martin asked. 'Respect for your elders,' was the immediate reply. He went on to describe how he had seen a younger worker strongly disagreeing with a senior missionary in front of other people. 'If you don't show respect for your elders,' he went on, 'you'll have no testimony at all as a Christian, and people won't listen to anything else you say.'

I once read a prayer letter which suggested the need for wearing (in our minds) a pair of 'L plates' during the first few years in another country. Everything is different and must be learnt all over again. Pre-eminently there is the language, without which one feels like a toddler, unable to express what one thinks or wants. But many other things must be learnt, too: how to shake hands, how to offer a cup of tea, how to sit, how to walk, how to say goodbye to someone at the door. The list is endless, and it can make the new-comer feel humiliated, even insulted. To be forced into the position of a child again, who is forever having to be corrected, can make one feel very vulnerable. If the new worker has not yet gained the grace of humility, this may prove very difficult.

Emotional stability

The unfamiliarity of new situations, coupled with the strain brought by radical change, highlights the need for emotional stability in the person offering to serve God overseas. We all function best in familiar situations, where we understand our own role and responsibilities, and have some means of predicting the results of our actions. Strain comes through the loss of several of these factors, and the greater the change the greater the strain it produces.

Our 'jet set' method of hurling a young volunteer from a wealthy background straight into a remote, up-country situation in another country can produce great stress. I noticed this when visiting a team of young workers in Khartoum. Those who had stepped onto a plane in Europe and only a few hours later stepped off into the scorching heat and impregnable, fortress-like houses of that great city went through a very difficult time. The few who had taken three weeks to travel overland found their stress appreciably lessened. Their journey had been a rough one, but they had travelled through country after country experiencing a variety of landscapes, cultures and different ways of life, so that by the time they arrived they were geared up to expect change and did not find it so difficult.

All of them however, commented to us that they had not expected there to be quite so much strain involved in living in an unfamiliar country. And the situation itself relentlessly exposed any areas of vulnerability in their own personalities.

It is comparatively easy in one's home-land to mask one's own weakness. We all find ways of covering it up or compensating for it. This is essential in our youth, or we could not cope with life. But vulnerabilities which have not been brought to the Lord for his healing form dangerous flaws. And these can easily crack wide open under the pressures arising overseas.

Emotional stability is essential if you are considering missionary work, and the Lord longs for each of us to experience this. If there are areas in your life which need the Lord's touch do not persist in covering them up. Confide in someone you can trust, and get counsel and help. The Lord's healing is for you.

Adaptability and flexibility

Arising naturally out of what we have discussed is the need for adaptability and flexibility. It goes without saying that those who hold rigidly to their own viewpoint and their own ways of doing things are in for some knocks! Unfortunately we do not always realise how rigid we are, because so often we have not entertained the possibility of other ways of looking at things.

We were all brought up to use certain sets of words to describe a particular concept. When I was young I frequently heard of the necessity to be 'born again'. Being 'born again' was synonymous in my mind with being a real

Christian, in contrast to those who called themselves Christians but had little vital relationship with the Lord. But when I arrived in Indonesia I found the local term to be 'Are you following Christ?' (which, incidentally, has a far wider significance). Many visitors to Indonesia dismiss the large churches as containing only nominal Christians, since many Indonesians give somewhat vague answers if you ask if they have been born again. But are these visitors not attempting to squeeze the church in another country into their own theological mould? The New Testament only mentions being 'born again' in a few places, whereas our Lord's usual command was 'Follow me'. A brief look at a concordance will indicate how often Jesus spoke about following him.

Similarly, we must learn to distinguish between what is cultural and what is biblical. In Britain we have a tradition of hiding our feelings and controlling our emotions. We might feel that to lose control of oneself in a fit of anger is definitely not allowable for a Christian. But we might allow ourselves the luxury of saying something derogatory of a person behind their back. In North Sumatra, however, one might punch a man on the nose but never gossip about him. The true biblical picture is that both are equally wrong (Romans 1:29,30). We must learn from each other's insights and not cling to our own false standards.

An appreciation of other Christians' forms of worship is an essential part of the flexibility needed to live and work in another country. We have all become used to a particular style of worship. It may be the one we were brought up with and have become accustomed to over many years. Maybe we have reacted against one style and purposely chosen another, feeling it to be more meaningful, or richer, or freer, or more spiritual. But as we find ourselves worshipping with Christians in other lands we shall find they express their love and joy and adoration in very different ways from ours.

An example: we may automatically assume traditional styles of worship to be unspiritual. We may have visited churches which we felt were dead, where (as we saw it) the pattern of the service was followed without there being any real life. Perhaps to us, spiritually minded Christians are those who express their worship in freedom — they are free to speak, free to pray, free to express themselves with their bodies.

This may be true for the church in our home country (though it is by no means the whole story), but these assumptions must not be exported overseas. Things have different connotations elsewhere. In some places, raising your hands in prayer or praise will speak immediately of Muslim prayer, because that is their stance. Dancing may be linked in the local peoples' minds with their old pagan customs. It takes a depth of spiritual maturity to see beyond the outward guises to the heart of the matter, to recognise true spirituality where it shows itself.

Adaptability, too, is needed in a host of practical ways: being willing to run your home in the local style, welcome your visitors on your knees if you live in Japan, and eat the local food, whatever it is like, with the expectation that one day you will actually like it! It involves giving up your own preferences with regard to clothing and hairstyle. A missionary we knew in Indonesia was strongly criticised for his foreign ways. One of these was that his wife did not have long hair like all the local women around her. She felt it was unimportant, but they felt distanced from her by her hairstyle.

To be willing to develop a high degree of flexibility calls for a spirit of self-sacrifice. It is not easy to put one's own cherished attitudes aside and voluntarily espouse a different viewpoint. But as we do so, we begin to grasp what a privilege it is to walk in the footsteps of the Son of Man. Through his incarnation he willingly exchanged the infinitude of heaven for our finite world, with its limited horizons. He voluntarily identified himself with us, sharing our viewpoint, learning to see things from our lowly angle. Only in this way could he fully relate to us, integrate his being with ours and be able to reveal the truths about God he wanted us to know. We are being called to a lowly form of his incarnation, to be willing not to cling to our own rights and privileges. If he, in the glory of heaven, did not grasp after equality with God but emptied himself, cannot we be willing to follow his example?

When you next have time on your own read through Philippians 2:5–11. Meditate on what each phrase meant for your Lord. Ask God that your attitude may indeed be the same as that of Christ Jesus.

A servant spirit

One of the striking phrases used about Jesus in this Philippian passage is that he took 'the very nature of a servant'. His own description of himself was, 'I am among you as one who serves' (Luke 22:27). And when the disciples jostled among themselves for positions of prominence, he told them that the greatest must be servant of all, giving as his reason, 'Even the Son of Man did not come to be served, but to serve' (Mark 10:45).

Is this our attitude as we contemplate what is God's will for our life? Service means giving someone else what they have asked for in a way that they will appreciate. So it means asking first of all, 'What are the people in that other country looking for? What are their needs?' So often we begin at the other end, stating: 'This is *my* gift. Now, where can I exercise it to the full?'

I remember a young man who had been designated to work in Indonesia. He was a highly intelligent person with a university degree, and his main interest was work among students. This was the milieu in which he felt at home, and he also saw the strategic importance of bringing the leaders of tomorrow into a living relationship with Jesus Christ. But the group of churches which agreed to sponsor him had no university in their area. They had little vision for evangelism, and they saw their main need to be care of the Christians themselves.

It would have been easy for this young man to have argued, 'That's not the sort of work I want. I don't feel it would be using my gifts. And anyway, I'm so young; will any of the older Christians listen to me?' Instead he went and did exactly as he was asked, being prepared to fit into their felt needs and their way of doing things. It was frustrating when some of the stipulations went right against the methods he would have chosen. But he had gone to serve the churches there, and a servant does not argue with his master. Over the years he won his way with those people and was able to influence the whole course of history for that denomination.

It is costly to serve in this way. But the younger churches around the world resent foreigners who come to dictate to them. They feel they know what is best, and we must respect their wishes. After all, it is their land, their church, their people. So a willingness to work under national leaders is essential. This requires a great deal of humility and patience, since they may well have different priorities from us and different techniques. But it is only as we go with a servant spirit that we shall have any right to minister to them.

If we have won their hearts and become thoroughly integrated into their culture, we shall find a gradual change taking place. They will begin to accept us as their equals. They will begin to discuss their plans with us, asking us for an opinion. The relationship will slowly change into that of partners in leadership. But this can only come when they feel ready for it, when they sense we are fully identified with them. Some churches where the colonial overtones have been strong may find it very difficult to get to this point. They may still have too many hurts to be able to accept an outsider on a level with themselves, neither above them nor beneath them. If this is so, our part is to continue in humble service.

But when we are fully accepted, a relationship of mutual giving can be formed. Everyone will find there are areas in which they can give to the group. In other areas they will be receiving. Yes, the local people may be more gifted in evangelism, since they know the background and culture so well. But we will have a specific role to play, so that together we are serving as equal partners in their land.

Patience and stickability

As will have been seen by now, the task of integrating into a foreign culture is a long and complicated one. Patience and stickability are essential requirements for any who want to work more than just a few months overseas.

Things move slowly in many underdeveloped countries. People may not value efficiency as highly as we do, so the processing of our visas (which is so important to us) may come low on their list of priorities. The erection of that much-needed hospital may proceed excruciatingly slowly because the labourers did not receive the nourishing food we ate in our youth, and their physique is not as strong as ours.

Maybe we also need to be patient with ourselves, as the mosquitoes hinder our sleep and our energy is siphoned off through the heat, the noise and the dirt.

'No one who puts his hand to the plough and looks back is fit for service in the kingdom of God,' Jesus said (Luke 9:62). The grace of stickability is essential for the missionary task.

When we first went to Singapore there was a married couple living there who had already waited three years for a visa for Indonesia. After another year of waiting had dragged by they returned home for their first leave and never returned. They found it too discouraging to wait seemingly interminably.

Soon afterwards, visas were granted more freely, and a great work of God began to sweep through that land. If they had stuck it out a little longer they might have been part of this revival. It is a failing of our Western culture that we get so impatient. We want instant results, short cuts to our goals.

I am reminded of the lady doctor who waited and prayed for eighteen years on the border of Nepal before she was finally allowed to enter the country. I think, too, of an early German missionary to Java, who spent eight years in painstaking work to translate the New Testament into the difficult language of Javanese. Eight more years were spent in printing it. This priceless first edition was then impounded for a further 17 years before he was allowed to distribute it. But praise God, he was one of the founders of a church which today can be numbered in millions.

Stickability goes hand in hand with the need for initiative. If the couple waiting for a visa in Singapore had grasped the opportunities which were immediately on their doorstep they might not have found the waiting so protracted. They had unlimited openings for evangelism. There were a host of young churches around them crying out for Bible teachers and trainers. Many people fall into this trap of living so much for the future they miss today's opportunities. I often used to smile at my younger daughter's frequent exclamation, 'I can't wait till . . .!' Why not get on and enjoy today?

Initiative is also needed in overcoming the problem of entry into countries which do not welcome missionaries. Last month we met a couple with a deep longing to help Muslims become Christians, but how could they obtain permission to live in a Muslim country? They tossed this question around for some time before they came up with the answer. They set up a small travel agency in a well-known tourist town. Trips up-country to investigate places of interest are providing them with many useful contacts. And quietly they are witnessing for Christ.

Spirituality
This couple have also become increasingly aware of the spiritual warfare in which they are involved. No bridge-head can be established in the Devil's territory unless the One who is greater than the Devil ties him up, restricting his power (Matthew 12:29). So the couple's greatest need is to maintain

and develop their own relationship with Jesus Christ. Only the power of the Holy Spirit can bring men and women to faith in Jesus. There is nothing we can do on our own.

Why is it that we still rush about in hyperactivity for God even if we know (in theory) we can do nothing by ourselves? Time is needed to develop our spiritual life. Ask yourself how many hours you spent last week over meals. And how many hours did you spend feeding on the bread of life which is the Word of God? Why are we surprised that we stumble so often and so easily in our Christian life when we fail to build up and exercise our spiritual muscles?

In our own homeland we probably have the privilege of fellowship with other Christians of our choice and rich Bible teaching at our regular meetings. But when we go overseas we may be thrown into a group which is not of our own choosing, and our inability to understand the local language will mean we derive little or nothing from the worship and sermons. It is important to have learnt already how to feed ourselves from the Scriptures. It is essential to be able to maintain a spiritual vitality in difficult circumstances.

The man or woman planning to serve God in another country needs to have developed the self-discipline of a regular time with God. Have you found a place for yourself where you can be undistracted and quiet each day? Choose a time when you are least likely to be interrupted, and spend time in the presence of God. Begin by worshipping him for who he is and praise him for what he has done. Reading a psalm or a hymn can often be very helpful here, or singing out loud. Give yourself time to become aware of the presence of the living God in all his holiness, power and love.

Then read a section from the Bible. It may be only a few verses, even just a phrase, or it may be a longer passage. Humbly ask God to speak to you through it. Expect to hear him speak to your inner ear, and be prepared not always to hear words of comfort. Coming into the presence of the all-knowing, all-powerful God can be an awesome matter. His challenge may disturb us. His love wants to change us.

His Spirit wants to expose and root out our self-centredness and fill us with himself.

If we long to be used by God in effective ministry to others we must dare to be ruthlessly honest with him. We should not be satisfied with a mediocre relationship with him. It is 'the people who know their God (who) shall stand firm and take action' (Daniel 11:32,RSV). Have we made it our goal to know God?

Final thoughts
Later we shall be looking at the necessary qualifications, training and experience to be obtained before setting out in God's service. But first I want to add one final thought on the type of person overseas churches are looking for to help them in their work

Sarah had been given the difficult assignment of working among rubber-tappers in Malaysia. She had been living for six months in a small village, attempting to get to know the under-privileged Tamil people and learn their language. The intricacies of this very complicated Indian language sometimes almost made her despair, yet she found the Tamil girls flocking round her home, and one day a particular friend of hers told her that she wanted to become a Christian.

'I don't know if I've even understood her right,' Sarah said to the English-speaking Tamil pastor as she asked for his help. 'I haven't really enough language to explain anything properly to her.'

'Don't worry,' he replied, 'I can teach her myself. But you know why she's made this decision, don't you? It's because they all see how much you love them. It's because they know you enjoy being with them, and they have so much fun in your home. Some of them have never been loved like that before.'

It is our love which is ultimately going to speak to people, not our skills or our cleverness or our training. Love is the key which will unlock the door of closed hearts. Love will teach us sensitivity to other people's feelings. Love will

sharpen our awareness of new situations and teach us how to
fit in smoothly.

Having described spiritual gifts in I Corinthians 12 Paul
went on to say, 'Earnestly desire the greatest gifts. And now
I will show you *the* most excellent way' (v 31). He goes on to
describe love, which is greater than anything else.

Before you sleep tonight, read I Corinthians 13 slowly and
prayerfully, asking yourself honestly, 'Is this a picture of
me?' Pray to God to grant a new outpouring of his love into
your personality. Ask that his greatest gift of love may fill
every part of your life.

Questions for discussion
1. Do you have to be perfect to be a missionary?
2. What characteristics listed in this chapter do you feel you
   lack? What can you do to grow in these areas?
3. Are you feeling inadequate? What did God say to
   Jeremiah when he felt like that? (Jeremiah 1:4–12).

3

What Route Should I Take?

Are Missionary Societies biblical?

'Many folks go out with missionary societies, but are these societies actually biblical?' a young person asked me. 'I mean, if you read the story in Acts, there's no mention of anything vaguely like a missionary society. Paul just seemed to travel wherever he wanted to, quite independently of anyone else.'

So we settled down to do a Bible study together. The opening verses of Acts 13 seemed a good place to start. They made it clear that Paul and Barnabas received a direct word from God setting them apart for a particular job. Certainly there was no mention that they were to found a missionary society. Just the two of them set out together with their home church in Antioch lovingly praying for them. 'But did God always speak so clearly and directly?' we asked each other. With a clear command it was easy to know what to do. Were they given a succession of commands?

We read on and found there was chapter after chapter without any other directive. How then did Paul and Barnabas know what to do? It is interesting that the first place they visited was the island of Cyprus. 'Do you know where Barnabas came from?' I asked my friend. As she didn't, we turned to Acts 4:36, and she was surprised to find that Barnabas was actually a native of Cyprus.

'Do you think it could be more than a coincidence that the first country they went to was Cyprus?' I asked. Pausing a moment to think, she replied, 'Well, it could have been that he knew the island . . . or he had contacts there . . . or even relations, I suppose.'

I agreed with her that we didn't know for sure, but these could certainly have been some of the reasons. We noted that after they had travelled the length of the island and reached Paphos on the western coast, they sailed to Perga, which would then have been one of the nearest ports on the mainland.

'Do you think that once God had given his overall directive he expected them to use some common sense in how they were going to obey his command?' I queried. 'I often feel he does that for us. It would be marvellous if the Lord were to give us a detailed blueprint of what to do, but I don't usually find it works out like that. What I do find is that we are given guiding principles in the Bible which give us an overall direction but we have to get on and work out the details of how we're going to do it.'

My friend smiled. 'I suppose if God spelt everything out for us he would be treating us like children, not like adults. What would be the point of giving us a brain if he didn't want us to use it?'

'Yes,' I agreed. 'And, of course, there were times when the Lord clearly intervened, like Acts 16:6,7. He is always ready to do that if need be. So since the Lord mainly gives us guiding principles in the Bible, I don't feel that because missionary societies as such are not mentioned in the New Testament, they cannot be part of God's plan to evangelise the world. If you think of it, in our Christian lives, we do lots of things which are not mentioned in the Bible — like having a birthday party or even a Christian funeral.

'Actually, we can glimpse a few hints that some sort of organisation was developing during the New Testament period; and I find these very intriguing. Barnabas and Mark struck out on their own at the end of Acts 15, but they remained closely associated with Paul, as I Corinthians 9:6 and Colossians 4:10 show. Paul seems to have picked out Timothy in Acts 16:1–4 and carefully trained him as they worked and travelled together, and only a few chapters later we see Paul sending him, together with Erastus, back to Macedonia, in Acts 19:22.'

We continued into the next chapter and noted a list of eight men from various places where Paul had planted churches who were mentioned as accompanying him — men like Aristarchus, Gaius, Tychicus and Trophimus. Searching in a concordance we discovered that several of their names cropped up in other places, giving a distinct impression that they worked with Paul over the years. In fact the more we searched the more we noticed that distinctive little phrase: 'I have sent . . . I hope to send . . . I thought it necessary to send . . . when I sent . . . (see for example Ephesians 6:21; Philippians 2:19, 2:25; Colossians 4:8; Titus 3:12.), and it became increasingly clear that here was a band of men working closely together and looking to Paul as the experienced missionary and their leader.

We concluded that the teams were spread out over a wide area which would have taken weeks to cross. Travel in those times was far more dangerous and communication less reliable and speedy. It might well have been the case that a more tightly knit society would have been impossible in those days. But here, apparently, were the beginnings of a missionary society which had an appropriate structure in that environment.

Independent missionaries

Some people, however, have felt God leading them to go overseas independent of a missionary society or even of a home church. And some of them have done notable work, such as Gladys Aylward in China and Jackie Pullinger in

Hong Kong. It is interesting to note that both these fine women were first in touch with a missionary society and were not accepted, one for her lack of education and the other for her youth. This could be a salutary reminder to missionary societies to be more flexible when screening candidates and to dare to take greater risks; I believe the societies have learnt from such situations.

Independence, as always, gives great freedom without responsibility. The individual may not be responsible to a home church, if they are unsupported, and therefore may not feel indebted to those at home. There is also no responsibility to the national church in the country where they work, or to a missionary supervisor. This freedom to go anywhere and do anything might appear attractive to some. But when it comes down to the nitty gritty of daily life we all eventually have to commit ourselves to some situation. We cannot have 'freedom' forever. We need to be accountable.

The independent worker very often finds it convenient to use contacts provided by other missionaries in order to gain access to local society. He or she often needs facilities which existing structures can provide and indeed all missionaries depend to a large measure upon them. When we were running a missionary language school in Singapore, all the independent missionaries came to us for our language cassettes and course outlines, and many asked for advice on practical matters.

The independent missionary must beware that they are not actually sponging off others. A group of our new workers arriving in Singapore by ship from the States told of an independent missionary they met on the voyage. He had bought a one-way ticket to Hong Kong, knew no one there and only had about US $10 in his pocket. When the ship called in at Hong Kong our new workers were welcomed by our local missionary team, but they found this other missionary sitting disconsolately on the quayside, wondering where to go. So they took him to our centre, and local Christians were eventually able to find him accommodation.

In telling the story they commented to us, 'He called it living by faith, but actually it was living by *our* contacts and with *our* money, because we couldn't leave him stranded there!'

To go overseas independently means that the national Christians have no ready means of relating to you. They will be familiar with the missionary societies working in their country and will know which ones they feel at ease with and which ones they find it more difficult to work with. But the independent missionary runs into the danger of not being accepted by the national church, which may never have heard of the particular denomination or fellowship we come from back home, and so may regard us with suspicion.

While we were working in Sumatra we learnt that a few years before us there had been another missionary couple in a nearby town. Someone asked if we had heard anything of their work, and we made enquiries of the church elders in that town. To our amazement we were told, 'Oh, we thought they must be Jehovah's Witnesses or Mormons, since they did not link up with the church.' We explained that the couple were Plymouth Brethren missionaries, and that it was the practice for Brethren not to work within the context of missionary societies or churches of other denominations. 'But how were we to know they were Christians?' our friends replied. 'They never came to our services or paid us even a courtesy visit. Actually, they lived here a number of years, but they got so discouraged they left, and the few people who had been attending their meetings either dropped away or came to our church.'

'What a shame that was!' I sighed to Martin. 'To think that could happen in a situation where there are so many opportunities to teach and preach we hardly know which ones to take.' 'Yes,' replied Martin, 'but when you think about it we were only accepted here originally because we were members of a mission and were willing to work with the national church. It was that which gave us our entrance. Without the channels which OMF provided we shouldn't have been accepted either.'

Of course, some people are sufficiently individualistic to
find it difficult to work in a team, and it might seem
necessary for them to go overseas independently. Some
strong personalities only really flourish if they have scope to
do their own thing in their own way. But most of us work
better in a team where differing gifts and personalities can
enrich each other and provide a healthy check for one
another.

'Tent-making'

Dr G was a young surgeon with two pre-school aged
children. He and his wife had a longing to bring Christ to
Muslim peoples. After some overseas experience, followed
by Bible and missionary training, he was able to get a job
lecturing on surgery in a large new hospital in a Muslim
country. No ordinary missionary would be given a residence
visa for the country in question, but his presence was
welcomed because of his contribution as a highly skilled
doctor. This couple were very sensitive in sharing their
Christian faith with colleagues and neighbours, but they
were constantly amazed at the opportunities which came
their way. Underneath the rigid, even fanatical, exterior of
Islam they are finding disillusionment and loneliness.
Through sensitive handling of conversations and loving
concern they have been able to share the difference that
knowing Jesus Christ has made in their own lives.

A talented science teacher, Miss M, was able to get a post
in a school in one of the smaller Muslim countries. It was
impossible to share her Christian faith in the school, but she
found that the local Girl Guide group was leaderless and
offered to take it over. Through weekly activities, weekend
camping and plenty of fun, she began to relate in depth to
these teenaged girls and soon found that they were asking her
about the differences between Christianity and Islam. Many
natural opportunities were given her to share what it meant
to be a Christian.

These two examples could be multiplied many times over.

Such people are missionaries in the sense that they have deliberately chosen to work in a foreign land in order to bring the message of Jesus there. This type of worker is often nicknamed a 'tent-maker', from the incident in Acts 18:3 where we are told that Paul supported himself by tent-making when he lived in Corinth. Such people, therefore, do not need to rely on funds from their home church or supporters, but earn their living in their own profession.

The advantages of this type of work are many. The foreign worker has an easily understood role in the new country. They can be seen to be doing an ordinary job like everyone else. People can relate to them as an engineer or agricultural-ist or whatever their profession may be, and this eliminates some of the suspicion with which missionaries are sometimes regarded. Foreigners who have no obvious job and no clear role may appear quite strange to the local community, but if you can say, 'I am working in such-and-such a job,' the local people will be better able to begin to relate to you.

There are also many countries in the world where it is impossible, or is becoming increasingly difficult to enter as an ordinary missionary. The Muslim lands are notorious for this. Communist countries have been equally restrictive. But with thorough investigation many ways of obtaining resi-dence can be found in such countries. Some enrol as students in the universities and so bring the influence of Christ into institutions which are training the leaders of tomorrow. Others go as teachers and lecturers where Western expertise is badly needed. Openings in most of the major professions can be found — medical, agricultural, engineering, etc. One of the exciting developments of this decade is that China, which for a whole generation has remained tightly closed against mission, is now asking for foreign expertise. During the tragic days of the cultural revolution under Chairman Mao, China sealed her doors to outside influences and fell far behind in the race for economic progress. Desperately striving to modernise, she is crying out for people with industrial and technological skills. The doors are now open

for foreigners. There are many agencies which channel
Christian workers into different parts of China, including
more remote places like Xinjiang and Tibet. But during the
long years of bitter anti-Western propaganda, religion and
imperialism were linked together and made scapegoats for all
the hurt received at Western hands. Christians now going in
must therefore be very sensitive and patient, not thrusting
their own views on others. Confrontational or aggressive
evangelism will not be well received.

The disadvantages of 'tent-making' also need to be clearly
seen before anyone launches into this type of career. One will
often be working in isolation from other Christians, and the
lack of fellowship and biblical teaching can be a great drain
on one's own spiritual vitality. The intensity of spiritual
warfare in a land which for many centuries has been in
rebellion against God must also be recognised. People called
to this type of work need to have a strong faith, and must
know how to feed themselves spiritually without relying
closely on others.

There are also practical disadvantages. Unlike members of
missionary organisations 'tent-makers' will not usually be
given time initially for language study. They will therefore
have to limit their contacts to the few people who speak
English. Or they will have to spend large amounts of time
learning the local language. As they are working full time,
their language study will have to be squeezed into evenings
and weekends, so that this notoriously difficult task will
become even more protracted. Coming in as a professional
also means that there is a very definite slot in society into
which the newcomer will be expected to fit. Unless handled
very carefully, friendships can often only be formed with
nationals holding similar status, and there may be little
natural contact with the majority of the local people. The
long hours which one's professional work necessitates may
mean that there is little time left over for other ministry,
which easily leads to a sense of frustration. The tent-makers
need to recognise that their witness for Christ lies in the way

they live for him in their daily work, showing his characteristics in their attitudes and relationships. And the fact that little help may be given by the employers in understanding the local culture may make the expatriate feel like a 'fish out of water' for a long time.

Because of these drawbacks, many 'tent-makers' have found it helpful to link up with a missionary society with a good understanding of the local scene. Some societies have systems of 'field partners', where people in professional work can be linked with them and make use of their expertise. Dr G, mentioned earlier, was linked in this way with a well-known missionary society. Before he left for his assignment the society briefed him on the background and culture of the people. On arrival the family stayed in the mission home for a few days acclimatising before beginning their work. They made use of the mission's language material and attended their field conferences for sharing of news and mutual encouragement. They were prayed for by the home supporters of the mission, could turn to them at any time for help and advice and also send their children to the mission school once they were old enough.

The present world economic situation appears to be adding to the numbers of people working outside their home country. Christians from Korea are finding themselves working on building projects in Kuwait. Arab Christians from Egypt or Jordan may be sent on business to Saudi Arabia or the Gulf States, where they may be surprised to meet Indian and Pakistani Christians. Young women from the Philippines are employed in many countries as maids, and some times have been significantly used by the Lord to extend his kingdom. British Christians working for the EU may be deployed to Paris or Brussels. Brazilian Christians may be sent on regular business trips to Portugal. It has been rightly said that we live in a global village, and nations are being shaken together as never before. We can see the hand of the Holy Spirit behind these movements, taking the followers of Jesus to areas where he is not yet known. And there are many who, after prayer, purposely decide to get work in another country in order to spread the Gospel of Jesus in that place and encourage the church that may be there.

Short-term work

One of the marked changes in attitude to missionary work in recent years has been the enormous increase in the number of short-term workers. Prior to this, intending missionaries looked upon their calling as a life-time commitment. Society was more stable then, and people were not used to moving from job to job. Travel took much longer, so that by the time you had actually arrived in Timbuktu you felt you had to stay long enough to make it worthwhile! When my father first went to China, he stayed 10 years for his first tour of service, and the normal length of time was seven years. When my parents left me for the first time at boarding school in the north of China, it took them a whole month of overland travel before they arrived at the hospital my father had been asked to superintend. With situations like this, if one was not prepared to give long-term commitment, one might as well not go at all.

But travel today is fast and safe, and this has opened the door to short-term work of all kinds. Operation Mobilisation (OM) and Youth With A Mission (YWAM) are two outstanding groups which are challenging young people to consider giving up a year or two of their time to serve God in another country. Volunteers are asked to do a month on a summer campaign, during which time they receive training in evangelism and then have plenty of opportunity to put into practice what they have learnt — on the streets, in the cafes, selling books and chatting about the Lord. Drama is used in open air and community hall evangelism. Singing, guitars and other instruments are used to draw in the crowds.

After the summer campaign and a longer training course the volunteer may be accepted for one or two years work and

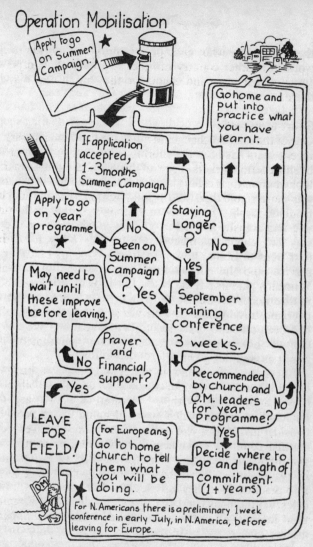

Example of application process when applying for short-term work

moves out to join one of the teams. These are placed in strategic centres in many different countries and work among a great variety of cultures and races. One of the more imaginative and daring risks which OM and later YWAM have taken is to buy a ship for evangelism and do tours in different areas of the world. The ship acts as a floating shop, carrying vast numbers of books in many different languages. It acts as a conference hall for large meetings, drawing together Christians of all denominations, in some cities for the first time. It provides display areas for challenging exhibitions, while all the time doubling as living quarters for the large team of young people from a wide variety of nationalities who live and work together.

A year or two training and working with OM or YWAM is a tremendously enriching experience. Many who have been with these organisations return to their home churches with a sharpened ability to serve the Lord. They bring a clearer missionary vision with them because of their newly acquired world-wide knowledge. Others find it to be part of God's call to them to give their life to full-time Christian work. They then need to do a full course of biblical missionary training before proceeding to long-term commitment.

Apart from the above largely evangelistic work, other forms of short-term work are available, mainly to those who have already gained some professional qualifications. TEAR Fund and a variety of missions channel into key positions those whose professional skills are needed. Some might be engaged on building dams or digging wells. Some might be able to advise on improved cereal farming or setting up a small livestock project. Medical personnel are particularly valuable and may be needed when more permanent staff have their home leave. After some tragedy has struck, such as an earthquake, flood or drought, short-term workers are often urgently needed to assist with the immediate crisis.

It should be remembered, however, that these opportunities for using skills will be very different from known situations back at home. For instance, we may be sent out as a skilled builder only to find the materials we are used to are unavailable in the other country, and we have to learn to manage with what is at hand. Our agricultural knowledge will need adapting to a different climate and local taste in food. The disease we will be treating as a doctor or nurse may well be a tropical one which we have hardly met before. And wherever we go we may find that the local people work more slowly (they have not been well nourished like us and may lack our physical strength). The heat may dissipate our energy and fray our tempers. 'Essential' equipment we have taken for granted at home may be completely unobtainable. Transport is slow and unreliable, since tropical rains wreak havoc with roads, and they are extremely expensive to repair. The work force we may have been counting on sometimes appears unreliable, since their code is that people matter more than things.

The short-term worker will find it much easier to work in countries where English is the language of education. When all communication has to go through an interpreter frustrations and misunderstandings can easily arise. There is an increasing number of places today where useful positions can be found for teachers of English. The Teaching English as a Foreign Language (TEFL) qualification is often essential here, and details of this course can be found at your local library. China is a country which is asking for hundreds and even thousands of teachers of English, and this provides a strategic opportunity for Christians to enter that country. If English is your native language this could be a God-given opportunity for you.

Short-term workers can fill a tremendous need, but this type of work does have its drawbacks. The temporary worker cannot expect to have any deep understanding of the local people and their reactions unless we are privileged to have the advice of more permanent workers or loving national Christians who are prepared to share openly with us. Misunderstandings easily arise because of the different cultures and different ways of doing things. It is very difficult to form deep relationships when two people do not understand each other's 'heart language'. Unless the newcomer is aware of local sensitivities, we may easily find ourselves setting up a Western-style project or unconsciously riding rough-shod over national feelings.

Understandable frustration is often experienced by new workers who, at best, will have been given a crash course on the local culture and language, and at worst will find themselves thrown in at the deep end with no initial preparation.

Yet an experienced mission leader once remarked, 'The advantage of short-term workers is that they are vividly aware of the need to train others. They know they only have a limited time on the job, so preparing someone else to take their place becomes their top priority.'

If you are considering offering yourself for short-term work make sure you are not using this as an excuse to avoid long-term commitment. And make sure your reason for going is not just the selfish one of 'it would be fun to live in another country for a while', or 'I do like hot sunshine and tropical beaches'! Are you going out there in order to give of yourself, your time and energy, or merely for what you can get?

Direct church to church links

Tom was sent by his firm to an Asian country to work for a couple of years. While there he began to pick up a little of the very difficult tonal language and to make friends with a number of local people. On Sundays he attended a small struggling church which met in someone's home a few streets away. After a time he came to feel that God was calling him to work full time for him in this Asian country, and the group of young Christians urged him to come to help them. So on his next visit to his homeland he talked it over with his church leaders. After much prayer and discussion they agreed with him that he should go ahead with his plans. The leaders put the suggestion to the whole church and they covenanted to see Tom through missionary training and to support him financially while he worked overseas.

Tom married a girl from another Asian country while he was training, and he and his wife have now been in their work for a number of years. There are very close links between the Asian church and his home church, which has taken on the younger church as its particular responsibility. The whole home church is behind the work in prayer and finance, and a number of its members have been out to visit.

Tom did not feel it necessary to go through a missionary society since he already had his contacts in the Asian country, and they had invited him to work with them. He was already familiar with the climate and some of the customs, and had friends who would guide him further. His home church was willing to take full responsibility for his financial and spiritual needs. Even so, Tom and his wife were glad to make use of language material prepared by the missionary societies working there. From time to time they spend their holiday in a lovely mission home by the sea, and they are grateful for the occasional opportunities of fellowship with other Westerners. Yet they are so fully integrated into the local situation that they gain their main support, socially, emotionally and spiritually, from their Asian friends.

Tom's situation is unusual, but it does demonstrate the possibility of being sent as a missionary directly from one's home church to work in a church in another land. There are also some denominations which maintain direct links with overseas churches rather than working through missionary societies. The Anglican church has chaplaincy posts in places as far apart as Cairo or Sao Paulo. Other groups, like the Lutheran World Fellowship, make direct appointments such as lecturing positions in Third World theological seminaries.

Recently, facilitated perhaps by the modern ease of travel, some Western churches have been forming close links with an overseas church. They may have met one of its leaders who might have been in the West for further training. Or some of their members may have been on holiday abroad and struck up friendships with local Christians. These new cross-cultural relationships can be tremendously enriching for both sides, as each shares insights and spiritual gifts and learns from the other.

The danger arises when one partner begins to try to manipulate the other. A new form of paternalistic imperialism can slip in, where Western churches attempt to manoeuvre other Christians into their own form of spirituality. Issues which have become very divisive in one country are forced into prominence in another, where the local Christians never before felt they were important enough issues to allow a split to take place. As one Asian leader remarked, 'We're not interested in whether a missionary is pre-millenialist or a-millenialist. We're far more concerned about a Christ-like character. But the American churches which financed the building of our Bible College insist we can only appoint pre-millenialists on the staff.'

Some charismatic churches are particularly prone to this type of missionary imperialism, hardly acknowledging spiritual life unless it demonstrates itself according to their own patterns and their own forms of Christianity. And this type of pressurising is not just an export from the West: it can happen from one Third World country to another. When we first arrived in Asia many of the Chinese churches were split following a visit from a dynamic actress from Hong Kong who insisted that the gift of speaking in tongues was an essential mark of the Holy Spirit's presence. The hurt caused by her visit was remembered for a long time and strongly hindered any openness to renewal movements for some years.

Not long ago a church leader remarked to one of our All Nations students, 'Our group of churches is not yet ready for pioneer evangelistic mission overseas. So the form of mission we are now engaging in is to bring the life of the Spirit into the churches.' Ostensibly this sounded good, but it raised two questions in my mind. Firstly, had they decided on this course of action because they lacked the patience and expertise for pioneer church planting in overseas situations, and if so, would it not help them to work with a missionary society with experience in cross-cultural work? Secondly, I wondered if this emphasis on 'life in the Spirit' would actually result in a divisive exporting of their own particular form of worship and spirituality, which would not be helpful for the building up of the national church in its own historical and cultural setting.

If Christian leaders bear in mind the above warnings there should be great scope for churches across the world getting to know each other in depth, encouraging one another and learning from each other. But let us not set up a new form of imperialism.

Missionary societies

The advantages of serving God overseas through the agency of a missionary society have already been touched upon. Perhaps it would be helpful to enumerate them more particularly.

Missionary societies can be of tremendous help with all the practical details involved in moving from one culture to another. They are in close touch with the situation in other countries. They know the personnel needs, be it for church planters, Bible teachers or a host of other specialist jobs. They can negotiate with the other churches as to what kind of person they would like to fill any particular post. They can also advise on which countries are open to people of specific nationalities. For instance, the French are welcomed in many parts of franco-phone Africa, and they have an immediate vehicle of communication in their own mother-tongue.

Missionary societies have knowledge of immigration procedure and can save weeks of time in the processing of applications as they will probably have personal contacts in various offices. Their expertise is freely available on practical points like what clothing is suitable, what equipment should be brought in, what can be purchased locally and what would appear too 'flashy' for a foreigner to possess. Help can be given with packing and transport and clearance of goods through customs. Different countries handle these matters differently, and local expertise can be invaluable.

Advice on language study is a tremendously important contribution which missionary societies can make. The enthusiastic volunteer often fails to appreciate how limited they will be until they have an adequate mastery of the language. We need only to ask ourselves whether we would listen to a Pakistani with halting English and a thick accent who was attempting to convert us to Islam! The acquisition of an easy, fluent and clear local language is the first enormous hurdle to be overcome. Missionary societies have been working on this problem for decades in order to come up with the most modern and efficient methods.

Over the years a missionary society will have amassed a wealth of experience which will be invaluable to the newcomer. In communicating the Gospel not only is it important to be fluent in the language, but it is also necessary to understand the local thought patterns and the mass of details which go to make up the country's culture. More experienced missionaries can interpret the local situation to the new worker and help in adapting to local attitudes and ways of handling matters. Even in small things quite a radical change of approach may be necessary. This was highlighted for us when one of our new workers in Singapore, having been asked in his first week to take over an English-speaking Bible class for Chinese teenagers, said to them, 'What would you like me to teach you about?' On being met with a respectful Asian hesitancy to push forward one's own views, especially in the presence of a 'teacher', he hurried on with 'I've made a tentative list in case you haven't any ideas, but I'd like to hear from you first'. His newness to the situation made him fail to realise that such a remark would shut them up like clams. It was tantamount to saying, 'I've drawn up my own plans; I'm just being polite in making a gesture to you first'. An experienced missionary, however, would know how such a group of youngsters would react, and would handle them appropriately.

The spiritual support which a missionary society can provide has already been touched upon. It must be recognised that on entering missionary service one inevitably also enters new dimensions of spiritual warfare. Our Lord referred to the Devil as 'the Prince of this World', and the Bible shows us clearly that he has usurped the authority which rightly belongs to God and set himself up as ruler. John comments that the whole world is under the control of the Evil One (I John 5:19). We should thus not be surprised that when we challenge the Devil over his usurped territory, he inevitably lashes back at us.

A few weeks ago I was talking to a missionary couple just returned from a second tour in Nepal. The husband was facing an operation. They were discouraged. There had been disunity in the team. And they were now feeling it would be so much easier not to go back. But was not this just what Satan wanted them to feel?

It is at times like these that we reap the benefit of being in a team. The encouragement and prayer backing of the small local team can often turn the tide. A visit from a superintendent can bring an outsider's spiritual wisdom and objective viewpoint into a demanding local situation. Conferences can give a new perspective and provide Biblical teaching. Here opportunity is found to sharpen ideas and discuss them with others, learning from one another. Many missionary societies also have a stalwart team of prayer supporters who have committed themselves to the vital task of praying for the different aspects of the work. Often it has been found that when a situation has been mentioned in the mission prayer letter or magazine, and Christians have deliberately set themselves to wield the weapon of prayer (Ephesians 6:18), the Devil has been defeated.

Which missionary society should I apply to?
Here are some questions to help you choose between
different missionary societies. Ask yourself:

Size: How big is it? Some people prefer a small society
where it is possible to relate to everyone. The family
atmosphere may be strong, with a consequent depth of
individual care. Some feel that the more 'go-ahead' ones with
a cutting edge invariably attract people, making their
numbers become larger, which gives scope for a wider
variety of personalities, different expressions of gifts and
freedom to exercise denominational differences.

Finance: How is the money raised? Does each member need
to raise a certain sum from their own supporters? If so, what
happens if you come from a church which is not very
mission-minded? Is the money members receive pooled and
shared out between them? If so, is it shared equally among
them all, from the newest worker to the General Director? If
just some of the money is pooled, what proportion is this and
what is it used for? What about contributions to national
insurance?

What is the policy on finance overseas? Does it tend to
keep the younger churches dependent? Is much of the
capital tied up in large institutions which are expensive to
run and tend to soak up personnel who could be deployed
elsewhere?

Theological stand: Does the missionary personnel consist
entirely of evangelical Christians? If not, have I found a
workable system for functioning happily with them?

Does the society make a clear-cut stand over some of the
issues which can sometimes divide evangelicals? For
instance, what is its view on charismatic renewal? What is its
attitude to baptism — infant or believers', immersion or
sprinkling? Have they a particular emphasis when teaching
about Christ's second coming? Is it a denominational society

with issues like church order and forms of worship clearly defined? If it is interdenominational does it really provide scope for the various denominations within it, or are they all squeezed into one mould?

What kind of churches does the society tend to found? Are they exact replicas of some church back home, or is the young church encouraged to be truly itself in its own culture? What stage of independence have such churches reached, and what position is given to national leaders? Does the society work under the national church, or dictate to it?

Structures and decision-making: To whom is the missionary responsible — the home church, the missionary society's leaders or the national church? Who makes the decisions? Is there a tight feeling of authority from above or is there more individual freedom? Are decisions taken by one person at the top or by a field council team? Are they taken by directors in the sending country, who may have little idea of the immediate situation, by those who are on the spot or by leaders of the country's national church?

What role are women given in the structure of the society? Are they given equal scope with men for teaching the Scriptures and counselling individuals? Are they involved in leadership and policy making? What sort of work are they doing?

Language learning: Is this a high priority as regards time and money spent? How long is allowed for this important task, and what standard is the missionary expected to attain? Are specialist personnel set aside to improve this aspect of the work, or does the mission mainly make use of language courses provided by others?

Efficiency and care: Does the society answer letters promptly and clearly? Is its literature shoddy or attractive? Are its conferences and meetings well organised and imaginative?

How much does the society really care for its workers? Are its missionaries given pastoral care? Has thought been given to where they can have a good holiday? What happens if they fall ill? How are the missionaries' children cared for? What sort of housing is provided? How much holiday do they get while overseas, and how frequently do they return to their homeland?

Every missionary society has its own character. Just like individuals they vary tremendously. If you are wondering about which missionary society to approach, as well as asking some of the above questions, the important thing is to get the feel of the society. This can be done through taking its regular literature (magazines and prayer letters), joining one of its prayer groups and talking to its missionaries. One of the most helpful ways of assessing the atmosphere is to attend one of the society's conferences. Here there will be leisure to listen to the speakers describing their work, ask questions of them and chat in between sessions. You will be able to see how they worship together and pray together, and get the feel of their work methods.

If you have not yet started to take a missionary magazine regularly, now is the time to begin. Their addresses can be obtained from the Evangelical Missionary Alliance, whose address is at the end of this book. Choose one you know something about or which is working in an area of the world in which you have an interest. And begin to pray about whether you should attend one of their conferences. As you take an increasing interest in missionary work, God can begin to guide you as to where he wants you to fit in.

Question for discussion
1. How would you summarise the advantages and disadvantages of going overseas with a missionary society?

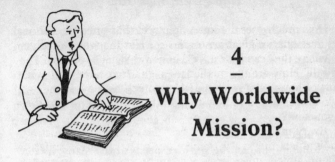

4

Why Worldwide Mission?

Common objections

'What right have you, anyway, to thrust your religion down their throats?' a young architect challenged me when I was a missionary recruit. 'They all have their own religion. How can you tell if it isn't every bit as good as ours? After all, Christianity has done some appalling things — burnt heretics, been responsible for tragic wars, massacred Jews — there's no way we are any better than them!'

'I think you're just being arrogant!' someone else threw at me. 'What presumption to think we have a monopoly on the truth! There is so much wisdom in the philosophies of the East forged over thousands of years. And look at Islam. Look at their pure worship of the one true God and the simple beauty of their mosques. They're every bit as good as we are!'

'Aren't missionaries just destroying other peoples' cultures?' another reproached me. 'They think their own ways are best, but they don't understand the beauty of other peoples' ways.'

'You're out of date!' someone else exclaimed to me. 'The colonial empires of the West are finished! Mission has always been linked with imperialism. The missionaries only went in riding on the shoulders of merchants and soldiers. Now that the colonies are independent no one wants missionaries. They have forfeited their right to speak because of the methods they used.'

As we have seen, some might add that since the national churches are the indigenous ones, they are better suited than any foreigner to take the Gospel to their own people. They know all the idioms of the language. They are familiar with the intricacies of the culture. Only they will know the most appropriate way of expressing biblical truths for their own people. 'Missionary go home' becomes the slogan. 'You are not needed any more!'

Some might feel the spiritual needs of the many Western nations are so great that we can ill afford to send some of our best workers overseas.

The thoughtful Christian, reflecting on the world today, can see how the centre of 'Christendom' has shifted. Britain itself is a 'mission field' with more than 90 out of every 100 people never going near a church. France and southern Europe have been spiritually dry for years with little effective evangelical witness. The whole of the Western world has become steeped in rationalism which has eliminated the concept of a God who is relevant and active. Materialism holds sway as the unacknowledged 'god' of our time, where an individual's worth is judged by the model of their car or the cut of their clothes. And paganism and eastern religions are making inroads and filling the spiritual vacuum.

A variety of objections to missionary work are being raised today. But also people feel keenly their own inadequacy to cope with this sort of life. 'I could never live up to being a missionary, anyway,' a number of young people are saying. 'I've read C T Studd's life and Hudson Taylor . . . all that super spirituality! I could never be like that. I'm just ordinary me! I get nervous if I have to speak in public. I haven't many gifts — at least not the important ones. And I don't feel I could cope with all those difficulties overseas . . . and Indian curries make my eyes stream . . . and anyway, I never was any good at French at school, so I'll never learn the language . . .'

Attitude of churches to mission
What, we may also ask, is the attitude to mission in many of
our own churches? How much is taught about mission here?
As one young man commented to my husband, 'We believe
in expository teaching in our church. Our pastor carefully
works through different books of the Bible in his teaching.
But there are so few passages on mission! Apart from the
Great Commission in Matthew 28 or a few verses like Acts
1:8 and John 4:35, there's nothing! So we hardly ever hear it
mentioned!'

Was he right? Are these the only passages in the Bible
which teach on mission? If so, is mission an optional extra? Is
it just a topic for the spiritually elite? May we ignore it if we
please?

Let's be biblical!
A hundred years ago the Christian public was challenged by
the vision of 'the evangelisation of the world in this
generation'. My own grandfather, Robert Wilder, was one of
the leaders of this movement. The missionary cause surged
forward on a great tide of spiritual zeal, and many of today's
large churches all round the world came into being at that
time and grew into strong indigenous movements.

But for one reason or another the edge to this missionary
zeal has been blunted. Some of the enthusiasm has waned.
How ought we, as Bible-believing Christians, to view the
topic of mission today?

Recently a survey was made of people who already had a
strong missionary interest. Among the questions asked was,
'How did you first become interested in overseas mission?' I
was surprised to learn that not one had replied that their
vision came from the Bible. Most had started to support
mission through personal interest in someone who had gone
overseas. Some had a particular interest in another country.
But not one had said their vision came through study of the
Scriptures.

I asked myself, 'What is wrong with our teaching of the Bible, that this should be so?' Does not Genesis 1 open with the profound statement that 'In the beginning God created the heavens and the earth'? There are not many gods, as some religions would teach us, but one sublime, omnipotent, transcendent God. He alone made this world in which you and I live. He alone made every living creature in it, providing a beautiful and fertile environment in which all could grow and multiply. And he alone made the first man, from whom is descended every nation upon earth. All peoples are his handiwork. His loving concern reaches to all races alike, without discrimination of colour, status or wealth.

God's unbiased concern and love for every human being

In the early chapters of Genesis we read how God's desire was for Adam and Eve to be in loving relationship to himself. All the animals and plants were made in their profusion of variety and colour, but mankind was made in a unique way. Genesis 1:27 tells us, 'God created man in his own image, in the image of God he created him; male and female he created them.' The very characteristics of God himself have been woven into the warp and woof of our being. To be human means to have the stamp of God upon us. To be human means to have been given the possibility of meaningful communication with the Supreme Being, intimate relationship with God himself. This is the birthright of every human being. And just as the Lord God walked in the Garden of Eden in the cool of the day (Genesis 3:8) in order to meet with Adam and Eve, so God has desired fellowship with every human being through the ages. God Almighty, the holy, majestic, supreme creator of the universe, sees reflected in each one of us a touch of his own personality, his own characteristics. Does he not therefore long for a special relationship with each human being on whom he has bestowed such a priceless gift?

We all know the tragic story of how sin came into the world spoiling the beautiful relationship between Creator and created 'image'. Our deepest being was marred by sin, so that all our feelings, thoughts and reactions became tainted by its presence. But this did not stop God loving us. The personal interest and concern which were there at the beginning never faltered.

God's plan extends to all nations

In the subsequent chapters in Genesis we read of God's continued commitment to our well-being. And when in his age-long purposes, God chose one man through whom to raise up a nation for himself, this was done expressly so that '. . . all peoples on earth will be blessed through you (Abraham)' (Genesis 12:3). It was *all* peoples God was concerned with — not just the few, not just those who knew him or had heard about him, or obeyed him. *All peoples* were loved by their Creator. Every single person on earth is stamped with the image of God, and he longs to bless each one.

God's plan unfolds in the calling out of the Israelites to be a special people (Exodus 19:6). Does this imply favouritism on God's part, or a rejection of other nations? No, the verse goes on to explain that the whole world is God's, but he picked out the Israelites to be a kingdom of priests. This meant they were to have the special task of acting as a link between the nations and God. They were to teach the nations about God (instruction was one of the primary tasks of the priests), and they were to represent the nations to God, praying for them and offering sacrifices for them.

Again we see God's beautiful plan spoiled when the Israelites sinned so drastically that as a nation they forfeited their right to be priests (Exodus 32). Only the tribe of Levi was given the privilege of Temple service, because of their zeal for the Lord, and only the family of Aaron were allowed to be priests. Yet this did not stop God's overall plan for the Israelites to be a witness to the whole world.

God's desire was that the life of the people of Israel would be so attractive — their relationships so beautiful, their laws so good and just — that other nations would long to join them and learn God's ways and walk in his paths. In this way the glory of God and the holiness of God would be clearly demonstrated in Israel's life, both as a community and as individuals. Similarly one aspect of the church's mission today is that people might see the beauty of the Lord through his people, both in our relationships together and in our individual lives.

Isaiah, early on in his ministry, had the vision of Jerusalem acting like a magnet to the nations of the world: 'All nations will stream to it' (Jerusalem) he declares in Isaiah 2:2. And what does he see to be the purpose of this? He continues by describing the scene more vividly:

'Many peoples will come and say,
Come, let us go up to the mountain of the Lord,
to the house of the God of Jacob.
He will teach us his ways
so that we may walk in his paths.' (Isaiah 2:3).

This is God's goal: all nations being drawn to the people of God, so that they may once more learn God's ways and know how to walk in his paths. The great Creator continues to long to walk with every man and woman, in intimate relationship.

Israel's failure did not thwart God's world-wide plan

Yet again God's plan was spoiled. Israel's life never reached the beauty God had designed for her. She should have been like a light, gleaming in the darkness, to draw the nations like moths around her. Instead, she was carried off in shame to Babylon, broken, dejected and crushed. Her wilful disobedience had brought drastic punishment in its wake.

Even so, God was not to be thwarted. His chosen people had failed him in their God-given task of bringing blessing to all nations. Instead of the failed servant Israel (Isaiah 41:8; 42:19), God would provide a perfect Servant, his own Son.

The failure of mankind having been succeeded by the failure of the elect nation, God now sends one into the world who will not fail. Seven hundred years before his coming, Isaiah foretold it:

> 'Here is my servant, whom I uphold,
> my chosen one in whom I delight;
> I will put my spirit on him
> and he will bring justice to the nations . . .
> He will not fail or be discouraged'.
> (Isaiah 42:1,4,last line RSV)

This servant who brings delight to God has a task to accomplish for the nations (not just for Israel). And as Isaiah continues to prophesy about him we see his work is going to affect the whole earth (v 4). Even the islands (to the Hebrew mind, the remotest periphery of the world) will put their hope in his law; in other words, every corner of the earth will one day come under his reign.

God's love is universal
As we read of God's irresistible plan as it unfolds in the New Testament, we no longer dare to think of God's loving care being for a few chosen people. Shortly after the birth of the infant Jesus, the aged sage Simeon, holding the week-old baby in his arms, caught a glimpse of what the Almighty God is about to do. He exclaims in rapture: 'My eyes have seen your salvation, which you have prepared in the sight of *all people*, a light for revelation to the Gentiles and for glory to your people Israel' (Luke 2:30–32).

Yes, not only the chosen people Israel, but also all the Gentile peoples now had the light of God dawning upon them. As Luke quotes in his next chapter, 'all mankind will see God's salvation' (3:6). No wonder that, at the outset of Jesus' ministry, the Jewish tax-collector Matthew quotes from Isaiah 9:1,'. . . Galilee of the Gentiles . . . the people living in darkness have seen a great light.' Galilee stood at the cross-roads of the world. Gentile armies, traders and travellers of all kinds traversed her fertile land. Through her the Gentiles would be given light.

John, in his prologue, speaks of the entry of this light into the world. He tells of Jesus' own people, the Jews, refusing to receive him, and then goes on joyfully to say, 'But to *all* who receive him, who believe in his name, he gives the right to become children of God' (John 1:12). The words 'all' and 'many' are theme notes of John's gospel. He goes to great lengths to show that no one is excluded from the love of God. 'God so loved the *world*', he writes, refusing to limit the propagation of the gospel in any way whatsoever. If the high and glorious God gave his only Son in order that *whoever* believes in him might have eternal life, how can we keep this good news to ourselves? How can we be so cold and unloving as to bask in God's love showered on us, and not move a finger to tell others that they too can become sons and daughters of such a wonderful Father? The Lamb of God has come to take away the sin of the *world*. (John 1:29).

Jesus himself took pains to prepare his disciples for the universality of their future task. During his earthly life he went out of his way to break down many existing barriers. 'No one is outside the love of God,' his actions declared. He straddled the great divide of his time between male and female. Whereas a pious male Jew would thank God every morning he was not made a woman and would refuse women all religious instruction, Jesus welcomed them. He consistently treated women as equal with men, deliberately took time to teach them and welcomed some of them to form part of his travelling company.

Jesus also set himself to explode the untruthful myth that some people were righteous and others were sinners. He showed up the pride and hypocrisy of those who considered themselves blameless. He gladly received the outcasts of society — the prostitutes who sold their bodies and the collaborating tax-collectors who sold their Jewish birthright for Roman money and favour.

Jesus also refused to be tied down by racial barriers. The disciples' animosity towards the mixed race of Samaritans ('half-breeds', as they would have been termed) was repudiated by our Lord. He would not call down fire to punish their insulting behaviour (Luke 9:52–6); but deliberately sought relationships with them. He spent time with the notorious woman of Samaria, and this led to many from her town believing (John 4:39–41). Note their words: 'We know that this man really is the Saviour of the *world*'. There is no exclusivism in God.

Our Lord recognised that he himself, as the perfect Israelite and the fulfilment of the Old Testament, had a primary ministry to the Jews. So he declared, 'I was not sent except to the lost sheep of the house of Israel.' Yet at the same time he showed an openness to Gentiles. He was willing to heal the Centurion's servant and the Syro-Phoenician woman's daughter in chapters 5–8. Mark gives us a fascinating travelogue where Jesus crosses back and forth across Lake Galilee, from the Jewish area around Capernaum to the strongly Gentile towns of the Decapolis. Jesus repeated for the Gentiles many of the miracles he had performed for the Jews eg. mass healings 6:53–56 cf. 3:10–12 and feeding the multitudes 8:1–9 cf. 6:32–44. Notice that with the Gentile crowds it was Jesus who had compassion on the people and took the initiative, whereas with the Jewish crowd the disciples made the first move. They were still only concerned about their own people, but our Lord's love was wider. In these stories we see our Lord was weaving a bridge across the centuries-old chasm which had existed between Jew and Gentile. And across this bridge his disciples were soon to walk.

Struggle against exclusiveness

Despite our Lord's all-embracing love and ministry, the Early Church had to struggle against exclusivism. The 120 followers of Jesus who assembled to choose a replacement for Judas Iscariot in Acts 1 were all Jews. Their upbringing had taught them to consider themselves the sole objects of God's love. The stretching of their horizons to include all the nations on earth was not without its difficulties.

The first explosive impact came on the day of Pentecost when proselytes to Judaism and God-fearing Gentiles (i.e. those who had not actually become Jews but wished to worship the Jewish God, Acts 2:10), together with the crowds of Jewish pilgrims, were exposed to Peter's powerful preaching. After the festivities of Pentecost they must have spread right across the then known world. The amazingly comprehensive list of countries is given in Acts 2:9–11.

Our Lord's careful preparation of his disciples made evangelism in the despised province of Samaria seem the next natural step when persecution drove many Christians out of Jerusalem (Acts 8:1). Deliberate preaching to Gentiles was more difficult, but Peter's vision broke down the long-entrenched feeling of exclusivism inherited by the first believers. As Peter exclaimed, 'I now realise how true it is that God does not show favouritism, but accepts men from *every nation* who fear him and do what is right' (Acts 10:34,35). So the apostles came to realise that the good news of Jesus should be taken to every person without discrimination.

The great commission

Each of the gospel writers brings his story to a climax with our Lord's commissioning of his disciples, that as the Father had sent him into the world now he was sending them (John 20:21). Matthew states this final command clearly, showing that since all authority in heaven and earth belonged to Jesus, the disciples were to go to *all nations*; in other words, the extent of the proclamation of the message must correspond to the extent of Christ's jurisdiction. Since he was King of the whole world, and his hard-won salvation was on behalf of the whole world, every person on earth must hear about it. Mark gives us his version of the same command, outlining the practical meaning of Jesus' promise, 'Surely I will be with you always, to the very end of the age' (Matthew 28:20; Mark 16:15–18).

Luke, who has given us two full books, has a beautiful linking passage between them, Luke 24:45–49. Here the risen Lord declares that 'repentance and forgiveness of sins will be preached in his name to *all nations*, beginning at Jerusalem, in the power of the Holy Spirit'. And this ties up with Acts 1:8,where Jesus outlines the strategic movement of the evangelistic progress from Jerusalem to all Judea and Samaria, out to the ends of the earth. So Luke, who at the opening of his Gospel saw salvation coming to *all mankind* (Luke 3:6), pivots his two volumes on the fulcrum of our Lord's command to go to all nations. He then ends his final chapter with the Gospel of grace sounding forth boldly and without hindrance from Rome itself, the capital of the world (Acts 28:31).

The whole Bible rings to this one theme: the one Almighty and holy God is the maker, sustainer and rightful king of the whole earth. Every man, woman and child is made in the image of the living God. In spite of the havoc wreaked by sin, God longs for a loving, intimate relationship with every person in every country. He made this relationship possible at infinite cost to himself. He sacrificed himself in the person of his precious Son Jesus, who relinquished all the sublime joy and supreme glory of heaven for our sakes. The perfect Son of God lived in this fallen world, suffering such incredible pain, emotionally, physically and spiritually, as we shall never understand, and finally made the ultimate sacrifice on our behalf by dying an agonising death on a Roman gibbet. Having been gloriously raised from the dead in triumphant demonstration of the efficacy of his sacrifice, our supreme Lord gave his parting command to every single one of his followers to go into all the world to make disciples of every nation.

Excuses answered

As we in the late twentieth century reflect on the command of the King of kings we dare not make excuses. It is true that

in the past terrible things were done in the name of Christianity. The Roman Catholic Inquisition perpetrated untold horrors against so-called 'heretics'. In return, Protestants have hounded and persecuted Catholics. Jews have been set up as scapegoats by self-righteous 'Christian' potentates and their followers, time and time again. The list of atrocities in the name of Christianity is horrendous.

It is also true that when cross-cultural mission took place in the past it was often linked with imperialism and colonialism. The missionaries of earlier generations had many commendable characteristics, but they were children of their time and reflected some of the short-comings of their era. But past sin does not cancel present responsibility. Previous attitudes of cruelty, self-righteousness or imperialistic pride do not remove our present duty to obey God's commands. We have not forfeited the right to speak. Rather, we are forced to repentance and shame because of the weakness of our forebears; and challenged to take up the task of evangelisation of the world with a new attitude of humility. We need to learn from the successes and failures of the past and approach our assignment with deep penitence and humility, relying on the Holy Spirit to show us his methods and to work through us by his power.

Let us also not be afraid of the jibe that we have no right to thrust our religion down other people's throats. We all know in practice that what is fed by force tends to be regurgitated! People of other nationalities and cultures are not mere passive recipients, but are perfectly free to spew back in our faces what they feel is being forced upon them. If however they find it to be attractive and valuable, useful in day-to-day living and meeting the deep needs of their hearts, they can embrace this joy by their own free will.

In fact, the phrase 'thrusting down their throat' is emotive and actually clouds the issue. Behind it lies the important question of whether we have the right to share the good news of Jesus Christ with those of other faiths. An idea held by many is that every nation has its own religion: Arabs are

Muslims, Indians are Hindu, Japanese are Buddhist, Americans and Europeans are (or should be) Christians. Stating it in this way we at once see some flaws in this thinking, since we know for ourselves that our own nation is by no means entirely Christian, and the more in-depth knowledge we have of other countries, the more we find a similar situation there.

Does the suggestion that each nation has its own religion really stand up to scrutiny? When we look at the biblical picture we see a clear statement that Jesus Christ is for all people. God's chosen way to himself is through Jesus. His death and resurrection have provided the means whereby men and women of every nation can be reconciled to God in his holiness. As Peter stated, 'Salvation is found in no one else, for there is no other name under heaven given to men by which we must be saved' (Acts 4:12).

There is no indication in the New Testament that the early Christians ever said of followers of another religion, 'They have their own religion; leave them to it. That is a perfectly valid pathway to God.' Rather, they took the message of salvation through Christ systematically throughout the Roman Empire. Even Jews who worshipped the one true God and followed his laws were told that was not enough. They should repent and acknowledge that forgiveness of sins could only be obtained through Jesus Christ and what he has done (Acts 2).

Other religions

What, then, are we to think about other religions? How are we to view them? Again we must consider the Bible's perspective. We have seen how in the beginning God made mankind in his own image; but sin came, spoiling the relationship between God and the human race. With the fall, everyone became corrupted at every point of their personality and being. Yet everyone retains a remnant image of God. This remnant image means each person is still capable of doing good, though their good will never be perfect. And all of us still retain the capacity for vibrant gifts of music, poetry, art, though our expression of each of these is never untainted by sin.

Similarly, God's grace has been poured out in general revelation to all mankind, and many religions contain elements of truth within them. Sincere people seeking after truth all down the ages have glimpsed aspects of it, but have never reached the whole truth by their own effort. Such truth as they have seen is always corrupted. For example, the Muslim belief that 'God is one' or 'God is all-powerful' is true. But their understanding of the unity of God and his sovereign power is sadly corrupted in that they deny the trinity and make God's power stand above his holiness and his loving involvement with mankind. The Eastern emphasis on mystical spirituality and meditation helpfully corrects an unbalanced activism and brashness in Western Christianity, but it needs to be seen for what it is: a basic contradiction of fundamental Christian dogma. Sadly, Eastern meditation denies the existence of our very being, and suppresses not only evil lusts but good emotions like love and joy. The Christian corrective to this can be seen in the God who revealed himself as 'I am' (Exodus 3:14), God who glories in existence and sent his Son that we might have life, and have it to the full (John 10:10).

Our responsibility

The Bible shows us that although there is much that is good and beautiful in other religions (alongside what is evil and depraved), those who follow them still need the light of the gospel. We who are followers of Christ must shoulder the responsibility of taking it to them.

We have Christ's explicit command to go into all the world and preach the gospel to every creature. How dare we conjure up our feeble excuses as to why we personally need not be involved? Our churches and fellowships are too self-centred. We are too absorbed with our own petty problems. Too engrossed in our own plans. Too hampered by our personality clashes. Too entranced by new fads of worship or ministry. Too distracted by the latest debating point on spiritual gifts, or Kingdom theology, or the place of prophecy and the land of Israel. These may be good and valid in their place, but if they detract from the central goal of Scripture they must be returned to their proper perspective.

The Bible reassures us as to the certainty of the fulfilment of God's plan. He 'works out everything in conformity with the purpose of his will' (Ephesians 1:11): 'At the name of Jesus every knee shall bow, in heaven and on earth and under the earth, and every tongue confess that Jesus Christ is Lord, to the glory of God the Father' (Philippians 2:10,11). And the final book of the Bible describes the great company in heaven, consisting of so many people that no one can count them, 'from every nation, tribe, people and language', standing before the throne of God (Revelation 7:9). This is the ultimate goal of history; this is what God has committed himself to bring about.

Are we prepared to stand on the side-line, to go on disassociating ourselves from God's pressing challenge and purpose for his creation? Are we content to continue in our half-hearted commitment, attempting to draw for ourselves the benefits of salvation but too self-centred to pass it on to others? The challenge comes to each one of us: What part am *I* prepared to play, what part has God planned for me in bringing the good news of Jesus Christ to every person upon earth?

Questions for discussion
1. Universality: God has an international purpose! What does John 1:1–18 say about 'the world' and 'all'?
2. What common excuses have you heard as to why we should not be involved in missionary work? How would you respond to these?
3. What responsibility does Paul say that we have as Christians? See II Corinthians 5:14–21.

5

How Can I know God's Will for my Life?

God wants to guide us

'We are God's workmanship, created in Christ Jesus to do good works, which God prepared in advance for us to do' (Ephesians 2:10).

Someone has translated the opening words of this verse as 'we are God's masterpiece', and it conjures up in my mind the image of a beautiful painting or an exquisitely ornamented hand-made vase. This is how our heavenly Father regards each one of us. We are his special work of art, individually created to give him pleasure, made with a unique purpose in mind, and beautifully graced with all we need to fulfil that purpose. God, who knows the end from the beginning and is lavish with his gifts and love has formed

76

each one of us to fit into a unique part of his overall plan for the world. He already knows all the particular things he has planned for us to do. He has prepared specific good things for each of us to accomplish.

Since we are God's workmanship, will he not show us what his plans are for our life? The Bible makes it abundantly clear that God is one who guides his people.

In the early chapters of Genesis we see Abraham being called to leave his own country and go to the land God would show him (Genesis 12:1). Without knowing his destination he set out, and God led him all the way to the country which was to become the homeland for the Israelites. After their protracted stay in Egypt God led the Israelites back home again. They could easily have lost their way in the desert, but God gave them a pillar of cloud by day and a pillar of fire by night to show them the path. And to forestall them being terrified by being forced into battle too soon, God led them the longer way round, not by the short cut through Philistine territory (Exodus 13:17,18). All through their journey we see how God was aware of the people's limitations and needs and so led them accordingly. He provided them with water to drink and daily manna to eat, and it is even recorded that their feet did not swell or their shoes wear out, so lovingly did God look after them.

Right through Scripture we see the unchanging God delighting in guiding his people. The moment they turned to him for counsel and help he was ready to give it. When they were attacked by Moabites or Midianites in the times of the Judges they cried out to God, and he raised up a new leader for them, teaching him new tactics of war. When David was at a loss what to do during the desperate years of constantly evading Saul's murderous intentions he enquired of the Lord, and the Lord showed him what to do (1 Samuel 23:1–13). Time and again, when the kings of Israel and Judah asked for God's guidance, he clearly revealed the right way forward.

Many of the Psalms have encapsulated this lovely side of God's character. Psalm 32:8 brings us God's promise to his people. 'I will instruct you and teach you in the way you should go. I will counsel you and watch over you.' And it goes on to warn us, 'Do not be like the horse or the mule which have no understanding but must be controlled by bit and bridle or they will not come to you.' This is saying that God longs for our free co-operation. He has plans for us. He has promised to make them clear. We must not go off on our own headlong way, but listen to God and be sensitive to what he is saying.

Psalm 78 was written to 'tell the next generation the praiseworthy deeds of the Lord, his power and the wonders he has done' (v 4). And among the verses is the oft-repeated statement that 'he guided them' (v 14,52–54), as if to make clear that this is one of the characteristics of God. We can take courage that what he did for the Israelites in their situation he will do for us.

The simile used for God's guidance is that of a shepherd leading his flock through the desert (v 52). Psalm 78 ends by telling us how God gave his people King David to be their shepherd, indicating expressly that David was their leader (v 72). The Westerner does not naturally equate a shepherd with a guide, since any sheep we may see being moved from place to place will probably be driven by a man or a dog. But the Eastern shepherd walked in front of his flock and still does to this day, picking out the path for them. As he walks in front he is not only showing the way, but going ahead of them, through all that they are asked to go through. So our Lord's statement 'I am the good Shepherd' should be understood to include his promise that he will guide his followers, and that there is no path we are asked to take which he has not already walked ahead of us.

The New Testament provides many illustrations of God delighting to guide his children. Joseph was warned to take the infant Jesus into Egypt in order to escape King Herod's murderous plots. Our Lord was led by the Spirit into the desert, showing that guidance does not always lead away from conflict, but may take us directly into it. However, since it was the Father's chosen place for the Son at that moment he could count on the Father's provision for all his needs. The disciples were guided to the upper room where they could eat the Passover meal with their Lord before his arrest. And after the Ascension they were instructed to wait in Jerusalem until 'power from on high' clothed them. The infant Church frequently prayed to the Lord for guidance, receiving his counsel and direction.

We too can feel confident that this is one of the immutable characteristics of our God. When we turn to him for guidance he will gladly respond to us. He loves us so much he does not want us to make a mistake. We need not fear a reluctance on his part to make his will known to us, or an obtruseness which will hide his real meaning in ambiguities. If we are praying over a decision and still are not quite sure what God's will is, we need not agonise in our uncertainty. More than we desire it, God wants us to know his will and do it. He has committed himself to guiding us. What are some of the means God uses to reveal his will?

Guidance through the Bible

That great man of God, the apostle Paul, shows us where our reliable source of guidance lies. He was drawing near to the end of his life. Increasingly he felt the cold of the approaching winter and asked for his cloak to be sent to him. Many of his fellow workers had scattered to other places to pastor young churches, and only the faithful doctor Luke was with him. Paul wrote what we call his second letter to Timothy (though there may well have been other letters), stating he was aware that his life was drawing to a close: 'I have fought the good fight, I have finished the race' (II Timothy 4:7).

What was going to guard and protect the infant churches now that the original leaders were coming to the end of their lives, one by one? Paul encourages Timothy with a reminder: 'From childhood you have known the holy Scriptures', he writes, 'which are able to make you wise for salvation through faith in Christ' (II Timothy 3:15). He then goes on to spell out the origin of holy Scripture and God's express purpose in giving it to us: 'All Scripture is God-breathed, and is useful for teaching, rebuking, correcting and training in righteousness, so that the man of God may be thoroughly equipped for every good work' (v 16).

Firstly, Paul states that Scripture is the very words of God to us. God has 'breathed out' the words of the Bible through inspiring its writers and causing them to write down what God wanted recorded. We have here, as it were, a love-letter from the heavenly Father to his children. Through its pages he expresses the things he wants us to know about himself, his character and his ways of working. He reveals to us secrets of how the universe came into being, why this world is in such a sad and sorry mess, and how we can enter into a living relationship with God himself which will lift us out of our quagmire and change us into the people we long to be.

Secondly, Paul shows that the Bible is the tool which God has placed in our hands to teach, rebuke, correct and train us in righteousness, in order that we may be equipped to do the good works which God has planned for us.

How can this be? How can the Bible do all those things for us? As we read it and study it we shall soon realise what an effective teacher the Bible can be, revealing all that we need to know. As we apply the lessons it spells out to our own situation, we shall hear it rebuking our own attitudes and actions. We shall be excited to discover how the lives of men and women centuries ago can challenge our lives today and train us in righteousness.

Some years ago my husband and I attended a service. The opening words of the reading came from I Samuel 16:1, 'The Lord said to Samuel "How long will you grieve for Saul, since I have rejected him as king?" ' The word 'grieve' cut me like a knife, since only a few minutes before I had used it to my husband expressing my feelings over a promising

Christian leader who had fallen into sin. For six months he had dominated my prayer life as I pleaded with the Lord to move in his heart and change his attitude. As I thought of King Saul, with all his promising gifts and the tragedy of his life, the similarity of the two situations was clearly etched for me. My husband and I looked at each other. We both knew the Lord was saying something. Grief had been right at the time. But we were now to move on. The Lord would raise up a new leader in place of the other man. There were other people to whom we must give our thoughts and prayers.

From time to time I have found the Bible speaking to me in this clear-cut way, with a razor-sharp word piercing directly into my situation. The word of God which the Holy Spirit caused to be written so long ago is still a 'living word'. It is alive. As the writer of the letter to the Hebrews describes it, 'The word of God is living and active. Sharper than any double-edged sword, it penetrates even to dividing soul and spirit, joints and marrow, it judges the thoughts and attitudes of the heart' (Hebrews 4:12).

The times when the Bible has spoken to me like this have usually been during my regular reading or study of it. In my daily times of stillness with God, as I read consecutively through the pages of Scripture, God speaks into my present situation. As we worship with others and listen to God's word being expounded, the living God communicates with us all. At times there must be quietness and waiting before we hear his voice. Some days he seems not to speak at all, and we must resist any temptation to attempt to manipulate him into declaring his will. He will speak when he wants to. It is our responsibility to remain listening. If there is a matter God wishes us to know, he is well able to communicate it to us.

The first time I remember hearing the word of God burning into my heart was when I was still at school. My sister and I went to the church youth Bible study. That evening our vicar had read the words 'You are not your own. You were bought with a price' (I Corinthians 6:19,20).

Whether he spoke at length on this verse, or whether it was read in passing, I cannot remember. But I knew that in this explicit statement of fact the Lord was addressing me. I was forced to face up to it; there was no getting away. Since I had willingly accepted the ransom price which had been paid for me, since I had appropriated it to myself, I had also taken on the consequences.

I cycled home that night behind my sister with this persistent thought drumming in my head. As my legs pumped rhythmically, pushing at the pedals, I could hear again those words 'you're not your own', 'you were bought with a price'. By the time we arrived home I knew I had made a transaction with God. Whatever he said to me I would do. Wherever he sent me I would go. If he wished me to serve him overseas as a missionary, I was willing.

We may all have had experience of God speaking to us directly through a particular passage of Scripture. But as we read the Bible, we shall not always find in it minute instructions for the details of our lives. This would be impossible, since Scripture was designed to guide not only people in the twentieth-century but Christians all through the ages, at every point of church history, from every race and stratum of society. This is why, instead of explicit details of commands, we find stories of how God related to men and women in the past, the lessons he taught them, and aspects of his character which he revealed to them through their experiences. We find beautiful poetry expressing worship and adoration of our transcendent God, portraying the intimate relationship which he longs to have with his people. We also come across repentance and confession, where people failed him. And we find prophetic denunciation of sin and warnings about the consequences of wilful disobedience.

God's intention in giving us the Bible is not so much to speak directly into our situation through individual texts. Far more its purpose is to open to us the mind of God. As we come to know God, and to walk more closely with him, we shall begin to sense those things which please him. We shall become more aware of the type of thing which is according to his will, and also what he denounces. This intimate knowledge of the mind of God will not come overnight. It requires time spent in God's presence, listening to what he is saying, meditating on the Scriptures, until we begin to see things as God sees them. Paul was able to say, 'We have the mind of Christ' (I Corinthians 2:16). He had walked so closely with his Lord for so long that he knew instinctively what Christ would want in any particular situation.

This may sound a near-impossible goal, that we should achieve such intimacy. Yet we are all aware on a human level, of the possibility of knowing someone to these depths. In Britain we have a television game called 'Mr and Mrs'. One member of a married couple is asked, 'What would your partner choose in a certain situation' or 'How would he or she react?' It is almost uncanny to see how, when a couple know one another well, one partner can predict what the other will do.

So it can be for us, too, as we meditate on the Scriptures and consistently apply them to our lives. Increasingly we shall be able to sense what course of action would please our heavenly Father in a given situation.

Over the years I have wrestled in my mind with the question of how the Bible guides us. There is a part of me which longs to use the Bible like an old-fashioned promise box. When I was small, we had one of these in our home. On a Sunday morning, we would each be allowed to use the special tongs to pick out one of the tightly coiled pieces of paper from the finely ornamented box. We would read out in turn the verse from the Bible which we had drawn, and I had a feeling that 'my verse' would have a special reality for me in an almost magical way for the coming week.

How simple it would be today if, when I needed guidance on some matter, I could pick up those tongs again and unroll a piece of paper spelling out God's clear directive to me. But it is not as simple as that. There have been moments when I have had an inner conviction that the Lord was speaking unmistakably to me, but usually I find that this is not so. Rather, I have to ask myself, 'What would Jesus do in this situation? What action, or word, would be most in keeping with what I know of the character of God and his purposes for this world?'

I have come to see that this is part of what it means to be made in the image of God: that we are given free, deliberate choices. God himself is utterly free, completely able to make his own choice. And he gives us the dignity of immense freedom, coupled with wide scope for making choices based on the exercise of our own deliberations and accumulated wisdom and maturity. If God 'breathed down our necks' all the time, limiting our choice to the one question, 'Are we willing to do God's will or not?' he would be turning us into near robots. Therefore he has set us the much more demanding task of seeking to get acquainted with his personality and his ways, largely through meditating on the Scriptures and on his dealings with us and other people, and then using our increasing store of wisdom and maturity to come to our own decision about how to act in any given situation.

So young Christians who want to discover God's will for their life and where they should serve him, should study the Scriptures to see what are God's plans for the world and what is the task which Christ has set his followers. A deepening acquaintance with the word of God will lead to a deepened knowledge of God himself and open us to hearing his directions for our lives.

Guidance through prophecy, visions etc.

In the early 1980s a young man told me he was worried about his brother, who was just six months away from taking his final exams at University. The brother's girl-friend had said she had received a prophecy. She believed the Lord was saying that he must give up his studies, that they should get married very soon and then prepare for the great exodus of

Jews from Russia, which some people had prophesied would take place in the mid to late 1980s. While preparing for this event, she believed herself called to be part of the pastoral team of a nearby church, with which she had so far had very little contact. As can be imagined, the young man's parents were very unhappy with the whole suggestion. They were Christians and had prayed much about the situation, but had no peace of heart that their son should cut short his course.

What should we do in a situation like this? Does God guide his people today through prophets, as he so evidently did in biblical times? Is the gift of prophecy a valid one for today, or did it cease after the New Testament period? If a statement is given as a prophecy, how are we to know whether it comes from God or not? Should we submit ourselves unreservedly to a prophecy like this?

The valid gift of prophecy: Intermittently throughout the Bible, various people were given prophetic gifts. From Enoch, the seventh generation from Adam (Jude 14), through the whole of the Old and New Testament, from time to time someone was endowed with this gift from God. Sometimes there were long periods when God apparently did not speak in this way, as at the time of Samuel's early childhood (I Samuel 3:1) and in inter-testamental times. At other times prophets appeared. Although their task included foretelling the future, their main work was to tell forth what God had spoken to them. They were those who listened to God, heard his words and passed them on to others. Women as well as men were given this gift and office (see, for example, Exodus 15:20; Judges 4:4; II Kings 22:14, Luke 2:36; Acts 21:9).

On the day of Pentecost, when the Holy Spirit was poured out on the infant Church, prophecy was one of the gifts given. This was said to be in fulfilment of Joel's words, 'Your sons and daughters will prophesy' (Acts 2:17, see Joel 2:28–31). As we read the account of that incident we see that the prophecy referred to must be the telling forth of God's message both in Peter's sermon and through the other languages given to the disciples. This was given with such power that the listeners were 'cut to the heart' (v 37).

Prophecy is mentioned several times in other parts of the New Testament. There is thus no reason to suppose that such a fundamental grace of God, given to his people over so many centuries, ceased with the early Church. In fact, if prophecy is taken in its true wider meaning of telling forth God's word, which we see in Acts 2, it has always been an outstanding part of the Church's ministry. Specific 'words of prophecy', as the girl-friend understood it, have also been received from time to time throughout church history.

All prophecies must be tested: When writing to the highly gifted church in Corinth Paul laid down clear guidelines about the gifts of the Spirit (I Corinthians 12–14). In Chapter 14 in particular he paid attention to the two gifts of tongues and prophecy. Maybe they needed especially careful handling, as they could be open to abuse.

Regarding prophecy Paul wrote (I Corinthians 14: 29), 'Let two or three prophets speak, and let the others weigh what is said.' Prophecy was apparently a normal constituent of their gatherings. When the Corinthian church met together they expected to hear God speaking to them. But what was said was not to be swallowed wholesale, but must be subjected to close scrutiny. 'Weighing' is the idea used by Paul, as a purchaser of some gold or silver article weighs it in order to ascertain how much of the precious metal it contains.

The church is to respect the fact that God may well speak through prophecy. But because we are all fallible human beings, the message from God may be distorted, both by the prophet's inability to hear accurately and by his or her own personality and ideas coming through, both in content and in the way the words are spoken. Therefore, the message must be tested to see how much of it is truly from God. Other people must evaluate what has been said.

The Bible alone is our final authority: The Bible is the
very words of God, and we see this from our Lord's attitude
to it. He referred to the Scriptures as 'the word of God'
(Matthew 19:4f; Mark 7:11–13; John 10:34f) and believed it
to be a revelation of God given under the inspiration of the
Holy Spirit (Mark 12:36). Therefore, the Bible alone is our
final authority, since all other statements are tainted with the
fallibility of the person who speaks them. All 'prophecy'
must therefore be scrutinised in the light of the Bible.

What light does the teaching of the Bible shed on the
situation of our university student? Here we need to ask
ourselves, 'From our reading of Scripture, do we believe that
God is likely to halt someone in the middle of his studies and
send him off to do something else?' The answer is that this is
quite possible. God can do anything he likes, but nowhere do
we read of someone in the middle of training being called out
by God into other work. Certainly the call of God comes to
people in many different situations, taking them out of their
old life into another. But what does God feel about training?
As we read the stories of the saints of old we see how much
time many of them spent in years of training. Moses was 40
years in Pharaoh's court and another 40 years in the desert
before God called him out into full-time work. Joseph spent
years as a slave and in prison before he was given
responsibility. More than 10 years were to pass between
David's anointing as king and his actually being given the
crown. Daniel completed his full course set by the
Babylonian king before God began to use him.

If we continue to search the pages of Scripture right
through to the life of Paul and even to our Lord himself, we
see that God is not usually in a hurry over training. Usually
he works slowly and thoroughly. So this aspect should make
us cautious in accepting the girl-friend's prophecy.

Then, too, the fact that the student's parents were not
happy with his proposed change should have flashed a
warning to him. The Bible expressly states that we are to
honour our father and mother (Exodus 20:12), and there is

no limit of time placed on this commandment. It does not end when a young person reaches the age of 18, as some people imagine, or even the age of 21. It is stated unconditionally that we are to honour our father and mother.

Now, this is not the same as obeying them (it is only children who are told to obey their parents). To honour our parents means to honour their position as those who brought us into the world and thus acknowledge the fact of our long dependence on them. It means to respect their commands, wishes and advice, as well as caring for them in their need. A peremptory dismissal of his parents' advice would constitute a flaunting of this command on the part of the student. Rather he should sit down with his parents, discuss the prophecy with them, and listen respectfully to their feelings about it.

The student's parents very wisely refrained from trying to force their will on him. But since he would not allow any discussion of his decision they suggested that they together ask God for a sign. His girl-friend had given as part of the prophecy that she should be taken onto the staff of a nearby Anglican church. So his parents suggested they all pray that if these decisions were in line with God's will, he would make it possible for the Anglican church to welcome the girl-friend onto their staff.

Some people hesitate to ask God for a sign, and certainly there is no instance in the New Testament where people were encouraged to do so. The Jews were actually blamed for constantly seeking a sign (Matthew 12:38,39 and others), and one cannot picture the apostle Paul asking God for one. But it is a valid Old Testament method of finding out God's will. Ahaz was told to ask God for a sign and blamed when he refused (Isaiah 7). Many people have 'laid a fleece', following the example of the timid Gideon (Judges 6:36–40). Gideon knew God was calling him to lead the Israelites to fight against their enemies, but his faith was so small and weak that he twice asked God to work a miracle with his fleece. In God's gracious condescension he answered Gideon's prayer and gave him the two signs he asked for. We may deduce that signs may be asked for if we feel in a desperate situation and cannot see our way forward in any other way, but they are probably only for those of weak faith. I personally feel that the student's parents were right to suggest a sign at this point, not because of their own weak faith but because of the girl-friend's immaturity.

I would also question whether it would be in keeping with the biblical idea of service for the girl-friend to request a position of responsibility in a church with which she had had little acquaintance. And actually her request was refused. It reminds me of the story of the young man who within a few weeks of joining a church informed the pastor that he felt called to a leadership position there.

'Fine,' replied the pastor. 'You hand out the hymn books each Sunday for six months, and we'll see how you get on!'

Christians today often forget that the Biblical picture of leadership is one of service. A newcomer cannot expect to be given immediate prominence. We must expect to serve in any and every way we can. And if we have proved by our actions and attitudes that we are capable of joining the pastoral team, it should be up to someone else to propose our name. It should not spring from our own suggestion.

The girl-friend's prophecy must be scrutinised along lines like these. If she is truly spiritual and humble she will be willing for a small group of Christians to bring the prophecy under the searchlight of Scripture, asking the Holy Spirit to weigh it for them.

Other considerations: I wonder if the girl-friend was aware of the very awkward situation her prophecy had created for her boy-friend. If he followed her words, he would have no hope of a University degree and at the same time go against his parents' wishes. But if he called her words into question and came to the conclusion that they were not actually a true prophecy from God, he would be casting a slur on his girl-friend's spirituality. The prophet who prophesies and whose words are found not to be from God is emphatically said to be a false prophet (Deuteronomy 18:21,22). The Bible knows of no prophet who sometimes speaks the words of God and sometimes is mistaken. It only tells of true prophets and false ones. If on one occasion a prophecy is found to be false, that prophet is labelled 'false'. This should make us very cautious about speaking words in the form of a prophecy. If we couch the statement in the first person singular, saying, for instance, 'My little children, I am saying to you . . .', we are claiming to be speaking the very words of God. As such they should be beyond scrutiny, yet coming as they do from the mouth of a fallible human being it is imperative that we scrutinise them. And if the words are found in any way to be defective, they clearly cannot be the words of God. The person uttering them is prophesying falsely.

Jeremiah has some stern words to say on this matter. ' "Yes," declares the Lord, "I am against the prophets who wag their own tongues and yet declare 'The Lord declares' " ' (Jeremiah 23:31). The whole of the chapter has some very salutary things to say on this subject and should be read right through.

Unless we are sure without a shadow of a doubt that God has given us the exact words to say, it is much wiser to preface our 'prophecy' with the words 'I feel God is telling me'. This displays the humility which acknowledges 'I too am a fallible person; I do not always hear accurately, or speak accurately.'

Related to this incident is the whole subject of the prophecy which various people claim to have heard concerning the Jews in Russia. In my first edition of this book written in 1985 I noted how some were prophesying that in the mid to late 1980s the millions of Jews in Russia would emigrate. I said, 'In the belief that this is about to take place, centres are being set up to receive them. How can we comment on this issue? The most pertinent comment is: will the prophecy be fulfilled? If it will, it is a true prophecy. If it is not, it is a false one. Time is running out quickly and we shall all soon know. But if the prophecy is not fulfilled, let us all have the courage to say it is a false one. The prophecy has proved partially true and partially untrue. Large numbers of Russian Jews have left for Israel, America and other countries, but the great majority still remain in the former Soviet Union. And the exodus did not take place until 1990 or later. Evidently there was a divine impulse in the prophecy, but it was also mixed with human interpretation. This reminds us that every prophecy needs to be discerned and not just accepted at face value.

Are all prophecies and visions therefore suspect? Because of the misuse of the word 'prophecy' some Christians today are reacting against any form of subjective guidance. But let us not throw out the baby with the bath water!

God does speak in many and varied ways. Throughout history he has used a wealth of different media to reveal himself and his will. He will never allow himself to be limited by our structures. There are many instances today where God has used dreams, visions, signs, interpretation of tongues and prophecy to indicate his purpose to his people. He knows the most appropriate way of speaking to each one of us.

In my 10 years of missionary work in the Far East I was interested to see how God used dreams to speak to people, more frequently there than I had known at home. Maybe this was because the Asians took dreams more seriously than we often do. God may have been choosing the appropriate medium for communicating with them. I have come to see that we in the materialistic West need to cultivate a spiritual sensitivity which Easterners often have retained.

The peace of God: As each one of us increases in sensitivity to what the Holy Spirit is saying, we shall discover a finely calibrated thermometer within our hearts. This is that mysterious commodity known as the peace of God. Like a thermometer, it is sensitive to its surrounding conditions, rising or falling as we remain in communication with the living God, quickly confessing any known sin and continuing in humble dependence on him.

To change the metaphor, the Bible instructs us to let the peace of Christ rule in our hearts (Colossians 3:15). And the Greek word used for 'rule' means 'act as umpire'. In the Olympic games there were umpires whose task it was to make sure the competitors kept the rules. We too are familiar with the umpire in a football match who allows the game to proceed as long as it continues smoothly. But as soon as the ball runs outside the pitch or a player commits a foul, the umpire blows his whistle.

God has given us the priceless gift of his peace to act as umpire in our lives. We need to be constantly aware of that peace. Some of us are so full of our opinions and ideas that we cannot hear the faint whistle of the peace of God being disturbed. Some of us have hardly learnt yet what it means to be living in such deep communion with God that his peace is our daily companion. Pride and self-assertiveness will drown it out. If we truly want to know God's will and do it, we should cultivate a deepening sensitivity to the voice of the Holy Spirit within us.

We live in days of noise and bustle, rushing from activity to activity. Many people fill all their waking hours with the sound of music from radio or cassettes. But if we want to hear God speaking to us we need to make time to be quiet with him. Some earlier mystics have spoken of cultivating the 'inner ear' with which we can listen to God.

If you are wondering about God's guidance for your life, set aside some time in which to listen to him. You may not be very good at it at first and so might do well only to take an hour or so. Later you will be able to extend this to several hours or a whole day. Take time to be quiet, focussing on God, on who he is and what he has done. Give yourself space to worship and adore him. Then quietly spread out before him your situation as you see it. Tell him all the details, and then listen to hear if he has anything to say. He may give you a picture, or bring a verse of Scripture to mind, or show you something to do. You may find it helpful to listen to God with someone else present. Their faith may strengthen yours, and one person's awareness may lead to the other also hearing something.

If there is a particularly important decision to be taken, time to hear the quiet voice of God is essential.

Guidance through circumstances

'How were you called to work in South-East Asia?' I asked a friend some years ago.

'It was nothing spectacular,' he replied. 'In fact, my wife and I were waiting, hoping God would speak to us clearly to show us what he wanted. But nothing unusual happened. I was a curate. We were really enjoying our church and the fellowship there. Our first baby had come. We had lots of friends and a great sense that life was good. But underneath it all was this growing interest in missionary work, and a deepening burden to pray for what God was doing in Asia.

'When a missionary speaker came to our church I told him of our interest, but that we had had no clear guidance from God to do anything about it.

'Look at your circumstances,' was his answer. 'Is there anything to hinder you from going right ahead? You're qualified, aren't you? You and your wife have good health. Your parents would not be against your going, from what you've indicated. What are you waiting for?'

'As we prayed about it,' my friend continued, 'we came to see that God had been at work all through our circumstances. He had brought us to the point where we were trained and ready. The curacy period had given us invaluable experience, and no family commitment was standing in our way. So we decided to go ahead and apply.'

During the process of applying God used other methods to confirm his call to them, but the initial step had come when they looked at their circumstances in the light of the growing inward pressure from the Holy Spirit to consider work in South-East Asia.

As we have already seen, long before any of us loved God or even knew him, our almighty Father was steadily working. He was making us ready for 'the good works which God prepared in advance for us to do' (Ephesians 2:10). What we sometimes forget is that a sizeable part of this preparation came through our circumstances. God himself chose the home into which we were born. He watched over us as children, overruling all the experiences we went through for his good purpose.

When God called Moses to go and speak to Pharaoh and Moses began to make excuses, he was running away from the upbringing which God himself had given him. Who else among the Israelites knew Pharaoh's court as well as Moses? Who else was skilled in all the arts of Egyptian learning? Moses may have felt he had made a mess of things and so had been forced to escape from the palace, but there was no denying his suitability above all others to represent his people to the king.

Through our own particular circumstances each of us was given special privileges from God. Perhaps we were brought up bi-lingually, giving us a gift to be used for God in later life. Maybe we had opportunities for study, for developing artistic or musical gifts, all of which may point towards our future sphere of work. Each of us was born into a particular type of home, in a particular social stratum, which now enables us to relate to people of that type.

Some people have difficulty accepting their upbringing and chafe against it. They wish they had a different home and a different background. I was talking to an attractive music teacher last week who confided in me that she came from a very low-income home. From the tone of her voice I wondered how she felt about it, and so asked a few more questions. With a tinge of embarrassment she described the small terraced house in which she had been brought up, and the shortage of money to buy anything but the barest essentials. With her degree in music, she had been educated out of that level of society, and yet in a strange way she still felt part of it. She told me she was beginning to come to terms with her background. And as we talked, she moved a good deal further, seeing that this was all part of God's active plan of love for her. She could fit in easily where many middle-class Christians would feel out of place. She is now ready to accept with joy that this could all be part of God's guidance as to what kind of work she should be doing for him. And she has accepted a post teaching music in a deprived area of a large city.

Unexpected difficulties can also be used by God to guide us. Time and again in the Bible narrative we see how God used difficult circumstances to guide his people. The fierce persecution which broke out after Stephen's death (Acts 8:1) must have been terrifying for those caught up in it. They knew the authorities were angry at the growth of the Church, but to take matters into their own hands and illegally put someone to death was another matter. The Christians fled for their lives. But under God, good came out of this hazardous situation. Wherever they went they could not stop talking about Jesus, and the good news was carried throughout Judea and Samaria.

Similarly, the antagonism and jealousy of the Jews in Antioch of Pisidia finally compelled Paul to say, 'We had to speak the word of God to you first. Since you reject it and do not consider yourselves worthy of eternal life, we now turn to the Gentiles' (Acts 13:46). The lack of response among his own race was an unmistakable sign to Paul that he should concentrate on his commission to take the Gospel to the Gentiles. Far from being discouraged by his circumstances, Paul could see the hand of God in them.

God is sovereign. This whole universe is under his control. He is the God of history, over-ruling all political events. His omnipotence and omniscience are able to weave together not only the mighty course of world history but also the details of the part that we ourselves are to play in it.

My husband and I remember feeling very disappointed that we were not able to return to Indonesia after our first tour of work there. We had learnt to know and love the Karo Bataks of North Sumatra and feel at home among them. A mass movement to Christ was taking place which we longed to share in. And the many new converts desperately needed teaching and help. But the political situation was such that it was impossible to return. By faith we committed ourselves to trust that God was in control of the situation, knowing that he knew best.

Years later we can look back and see that God was caring for his Karo Batak church, and he was also guiding us in our development. The other varieties of work which then opened up to us enriched us tremendously. During the ten years we were priviledged to spend in S.E. Asia we learnt to relate to all the major religions of the world. This has been a tremendous asset in our more recent task of lecturing for over two decades at All Nations Christian College and preparing others for missionary service. Now that we stand back from it, what appeared to be an incoherent jigsaw at the time, reveals God's carefully planned pattern and design.

We have a gifted friend who is lecturing in a Third World theological seminary. It was hard for her when she first went out because her father was strongly opposed to her plans. This, however, led to her missionary society taking tremendous care over her parents, visiting them, writing to them and delaying their daughter's departure. The love shown and their daughter's dedication led to the father coming to know Christ.

After some happy and useful years of teaching our friend's father died and she had to return home to care for her widowed mother. The situation was very complicated. Not only was there the grief of a tragic bereavement, but the family had to move from their tenant farm, dispose of a fine

herd of cows and find a new home to live in. The deep sorrow
felt at such a time could easily have become mixed with
frustration at seemingly unending legal tangles, and anger at
being taken away from the work she loved and which God
had given to her. Looking back she can say with deep
confidence that all these circumstances were under God's
control. There is no 'second best' place for his children in
our Father's economy. Even when our life is plunged into
sorrow, and interminable complications threaten to sap our
strength, God is with us in it. The Lord used that time to
teach her many lessons and to deepen her relationship with
her mother.

Difficult circumstances are not to be fought against or run
away from. They are part of God's guidance in our lives.

When seeking to know God's will, then, we should take
stock of our circumstances and ask God to show us what he is
indicating through them. They may be blocking the
possibility of our doing something we had set our heart on. If
so, spread the situation out before God in prayer and give
him sole responsibility for it. If Satan is hindering God's will,
the Lord has shown us that through prayer we can defeat
Satan. If after prayer the blockage still remains, we can take
it that God knows what he is doing. In his love, he is allowing
the situation. We must accept it by faith, not fearfully but in
joyful anticipation to see what the Lord has to teach us in it.

Conversely, if circumstances leave a door wide open to us
we should ask God whether this is an indication of his will.
We must search our hearts to see that we are not moving
forwards from wrong motives or with a sinful attitude. In
prayerful dependence on the Lord we should begin to move,
asking that he indicate if we are wrong.

Isaiah 30:21 tells us, 'Your ears shall hear a word behind
you saying, "This is the way, walk in it, when you turn to the
right or when you turn to the left" '(RSV). It often appears
to be the case that as we move forward, the Lord speaks
to confirm our actions or to correct us. Someone once
remarked, 'You cannot guide a stationary car. You must

switch on, get into gear and begin to move forward.' Might God be waiting for you to begin to move? He is challenging you about the needs of the world. Your circumstances are such that you can do something about it. Begin to move, and expect the gentle voice of the Holy Spirit to indicate the true way, if you are turning off from God's path to the right or to the left.

Confirmation is often given from the time when we decide to do something positive. When, after a long period of much uncertainty, Martin agreed to join the ANCC staff and so had to resign from OMF, many things around us began to fall into place. We found a house easily. The children got into a good school. Starting from scratch, all the furniture we needed was found. And we had that sense that at last peace and cohesion were beginning to · replace our feelings of unease. As we took the step, God acted through our circumstances and gave us clear confirmation that our decision was according to his will.

Guidance through the advice of others

As this century draws to a close Christians in the West are learning a lesson which the African and Asian churches had grasped long ago. They are seeing the short-sightedness of an over-emphasis on individualism. The nineteenth and early twentieth century bred rugged men and women who 'did their own thing'. In the United States, the wide areas of unexplored territory necessitated individual initiative and self-reliance. In Europe, the spirit of colonialism encouraged lives of adventure and independent action. In the industrial world new inventions opened up the way for individual enterprise, so that the person who could forge ahead with their own ideas was the one who made their mark.

But this is not the biblical picture of the Church. We are all the body of Christ, and as such are inextricably linked to one another. What I do affects others, and their attitudes, words and actions affect me. We belong to one another and are responsible for one another. The answer to Cain's

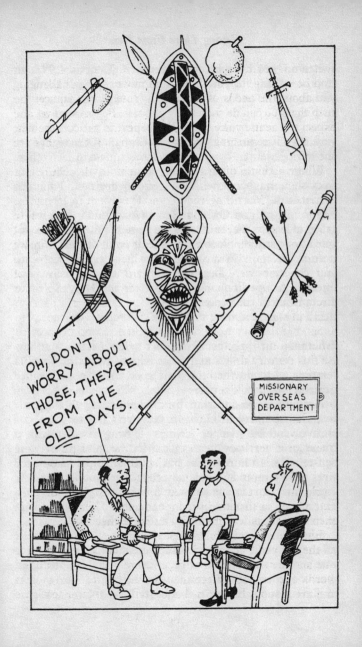

question, 'Am I my brother's keeper?' (Genesis 4:9) is an emphatic 'Yes!'. We are told to 'carry each other's burdens' (Galatians 6:2) and to 'strive side by side for the faith of the gospel' (Philippians 1:27,RSV). This is expressed in the Apostles' Creed by the words 'we believe in the communion of saints'. It means that within the Church of Christ, we are not independent individuals but closely linked to each other.

When a sharp disagreement occured in the church in Antioch it was dealt with by a group decision. Paul and Barnabas did not act on their own. They went to Jerusalem to consult the apostles and elders (Acts 15:2). The whole group of leaders met to discuss the matter (v 6), and time was given for many people to express their point of view. Finally a united decision was arrived at which was agreeable to everyone present. The way forward was thrashed out through group discussion, relying on the Holy Spirit to direct them in the process (v 28).

In the individualistic society of today we need to remember that our Lord said he would be especially present 'where two or three come together in my name' (Matthew 18:20). As we think about what type of work the Lord is wanting us to do for him, it is good to meet with other Christians and talk it over.

It might be best to start by discussing it with a friend. Friends are likely to know us very well and to sense our motives and our deeper feelings. Having aired it with a friend, the next person to talk to is the minister of your church. He is the one who has spiritual responsibility for you, and he should be able to judge where your gifts lie. If your minister is unsympathetic to missionary work or you have any other strong reason for not going to him, you can go to some other older, mature Christian to discuss the matter.

Some Bible colleges run what is called a 'guidance clinic', where two or three members of staff set aside time to meet with a student and talk over their future plans. Having more than one older Christian present can shed a great deal of light on the situation. Each member of staff has different insights which together can bring combined wisdom to the student's situation. One person's thoughts spark off new ideas in another person's mind, and so the Holy Spirit leads the group together. It is often amazing how seemingly very unclear situations become quite obvious when such groups come before the Lord together.

Churches which have a pastoral committee could share the load of responsibility with the minister by assisting in this way.

Another group of people to approach would be the leaders of a missionary society. They have first-hand experience of work overseas and know well what type of person the overseas church would welcome. They will be only too pleased to discuss with you whether there might be a suitable slot for you in their work, provided you are giving it serious thought.

Quite apart from a young person approaching their minister or the leaders of a missionary society, the New Testament also indicates the reverse taking place. Paul, the senior experienced missionary, got to know Timothy, a young believer, when he revisited Lystra (Acts 16:1–3) and invited him to join his company, giving him the privilege of training for Christian service under that great apostle. Might this indicate that Christian leaders should be on the look-out for young people of potential whom they could train? Sometimes we place too much emphasis on the young person feeling 'called of God' rather than the mature worker looking for promising assistants.

Of course it is possible for leaders to become too autocratic, and for some Christians through insecurity to become too submissive and so to look to others to tell them what to do. Emphasising the authority of leaders in a church can lead to the individual not having an adequate say in their own decisions. The Bible shows us that each person is answerable to God for their own actions. We all have direct access to God and can expect to hear his voice. He has made us a kingdom of priests, which means each one of us has a priest's right to go into the presence of our God and have direct dealings with him.

Tensions can arise between a leader's directives and an individual's own inclinations. These were dealt with in the missionary society with which I served by what we called 'guidance by consensus'. If an individual missionary felt led to do something, they submitted it to their leaders. If they in turn felt they had a directive for the missionary from God, they would share it. Both sides would pray about the suggestion until they came to an agreement which they felt at peace about. The individual was not free to act independently of their leaders, neither were they free to impose their will on the individual. Through prayer and discussion each party recognised the other's spirituality, and each was open to the wisdom and common sense of the other.

One of the tests to which we should submit our sense of guidance is to ask 'Am I being selfish?' We so easily deceive ourselves that what we wish to do is the Lord's will, but we are really only seeing our own point of view. Maybe our home church is going through a time of difficulty and crisis, so we choose to opt out and go to the more lively fellowship a few miles away. But were we really being guided by the Lord, or was it our own selfish longing to be in a 'successful' church and to be fed spiritually?

Perhaps a year in the South of France doing a specialist form of evangelism sounds attractive. But our younger brother or sister has reached a critical stage in spiritual development and needs us at home. Our Lord castigated those in his time who salved their consciences over their unfulfilled duty to their parents by saying 'Corban' (Mark 7:9–13). Dedicating money, time or anything else to God when it actually belongs to someone else (in this case our family) is not living as responsible Christians.

So be prepared, when you go to others for advice, to have them challenge your motives. Be scrupulously honest with yourself and with others. The plans you make will have repercussions for all those around you. Particularly it will be of great significance to your family, but it will also affect your work-mates, friends and fellow church members.

Conditions for guidance

The challenge of the needs of the world stares us in the face. God has given his all to save mankind from the results of sin. Opportunities to make the Gospel known extend throughout the world, and God has a place for each one of us in his scheme of salvation.

We have seen that God wants to guide us and he has given us many ways of discerning his will. The Bible forms our major source of revelation and ultimate final authority. Together with his word, God uses circumstances to guide us, our own wisdom and common sense, the advice and counsel of other Christians and a variety of other means, such as a word of knowledge or prophecy, dreams and visions.

But if we want to know God's guidance in our lives it is important that we do not hinder him. An attitude of pride may prevent us hearing his guidance. Psalm 25:9 tells us, 'He guides the humble in what is right and teaches them his way.' Often the Lord has to deal with our pride first before he can get through to us. So if God has been chastening you recently, do not feel discouraged. This may be preparation for a wonderful new task he wants to give you.

Disobedience may also form a barrier to guidance. If the Lord keeps speaking to us about something and we refuse to do it, his voice will grow fainter. If we keep putting off doing a specific thing, the prompting of the Holy Spirit to do it will come less frequently. Sin can actually quench the Spirit. Sin comes between us and God, forming a blockage so that we cannot hear him. God may have challenged us years ago to total commitment to him, but we still persist in giving him only half-hearted allegiance. There are areas of our life we are still holding back from him. How can he move us on until these areas have been dealt with?

Are you willing to do anything the Lord asks of you? Are you willing to go anywhere he sends you? Take yourself to a

quiet place alone with God and dare to ask the Holy Spirit to
search your life. Ask him to reveal to you any areas of fear,
reluctance or hesitancy, any way in which you are not being
utterly obedient. 'The fear of the Lord is the beginning of
knowledge' (Proverbs 1:7). Do you know what it is to fear
God, to stand in the presence of the Holy One with a sense of
awe and worship? Take time to do this.

When a close relationship with our Lord has been re-
established, we must keep ourselves constantly in tune with
him. Just as a pilot needs to be in constant radio touch with
the airport when landing, so we should be constantly in
prayer. 'Pray continually,' was Paul's instruction in I
Thessalonians 5:17, and I believe he meant we should
cultivate a continual openness to God, all the time, whatever
we are doing. We should have an attitude of expectant
listening, so that when God wants to guide us we are ready to
hear and respond to him.

Questions for discussion

1. How does God speak to us today?
2. How do we discern between God speaking, the Devil
   speaking, the pressure of other people's opinions, and
   our own ideas and feelings?
3. Should a Christian wait for a 'special call' before going
   overseas?

6

How should I prepare?

Some years ago my husband visited an African country to speak at a conference. Before returning home he had the opportunity of a private interview with the local archbishop. Among other questions Martin asked him, 'What sort of missionaries would you welcome to help in your church?'

The archbishop replied, 'I would look for three things: someone of maturity, with skills which are of practical use, and with a servant spirit.'

His reply fitted in closely with what we had heard in many of the Asian countries. As these churches are developing their own often well-qualified leadership, they require the expatriate to slot into positions which they themselves sometimes cannot fill. On the whole they are not looking for inexperienced youngsters but for men and women with qualifications and maturity, yet who are ready to work under their direction.

Maturity

The complex overseas situation necessitates a considerable degree of maturity in the prospective new worker. Political situations often call for tact and skill. We were the first missionaries to work in our area of Sumatra after the Indonesian War of Independence. It was very important that we behaved circumspectly with regard to all government departments. Missionaries will often find themselves in places of political tension, with rioting and looting going on around them. Many have to face civil war, with its ensuing complete breakdown of law and order and resulting terror. No good general would place his new recruits in the front line. He would call for experienced, tried personnel.

Being able to relate to the national churches also requires a degree of maturity. Their structures may be entirely different from ours, as can often be seen, for instance, in how a decision is reached. They may feel it expedient to maintain links which we would rather see cut and to cut links which we would prefer to maintain. The missionary will need great wisdom to understand their internal problems, and to maintain right attitudes without appearing to take sides.

How is maturity acquired?

There is no easy answer to this question. Maturity comes largely through life. It cannot be artificially stitched on like a patch on a garment. It can only grow quietly and steadily as one's own personality grows. Often the most difficult times of life are the ones which produce maturity: those experiences of disappointment or frustration which make us feel as if we were moving backwards, not forwards. The things which try our patience, the situations which are beyond our control and which we think will overwhelm us, actually teach us lessons far deeper than any textbook. Suffering is one of God's instruments to mature and refine us. Some people seem to sail through life, whereas others face one difficulty after another.

I have a young friend, just nineteen years old. Her parents never made it easy for her to be a Christian, as they were afraid she would become fanatical. They opposed her going to the young people's fellowship, so that for a long while she received little encouragement from others. Then her father was made redundant, and this increased the tension at home. Recently she broke her leg in a motor-bike accident, and for a time the doctors feared she would always walk with a limp. But I can see how all these difficulties have actually been refining her. She has a quality about her which is beautiful, and when her opinion is sought, the maturity which her experiences have created shines with depth.

Experience of ordinary life and human problems is important. Young people who have passed straight from school to college or university seldom have an awareness of what real life is all about. If their financial needs have been met all the way through by parents and then by a college grant, they will have little insight into the problems of a wage-earner. Several years working hard and earning your own living will give invaluable experience. You will gain understanding into the pressures and tensions the men and women around you are facing. Talk with people and try to get them to open up about the difficulties they experience. Gain insight into their conflicting pressures at work, how they tie these in with family demands and the need for relaxation. Working alongside others you too will experience these tensions and discover how to find God's strength and guidance in the details of daily living.

Relating to others: Growing in ability to relate to others is another key factor. Very often the root problem in any conflict is not the conditions of work or the hours required but the relationship between the people involved. We label and classify others according to their position, or a chance remark we overheard, or their style of clothes, and fail to appreciate the complex individuals beneath the exterior. We miss what they are trying to say by imposing our own ideas and jumping to conclusions. The end result is either a withdrawal in order to protect ourselves or a locking into battle.

But if we have not learnt to relate to people in our own culture and using our own language, how will we manage overseas? One of the main problems missionary superintendents have to deal with is interpersonal relationships. For example, there may be a married couple with three pre-school children, working on an agricultural project. A single lady missionary is sent to assist at the Bible School down the road. She begins to feel lonely as she has no one to unburden herself to, and the missionary wife is far too tired to listen. Jealousy creeps in as the wife sees her husband and the single girl begin to relate to one another, and he becomes critical of his wife and the way she runs the home. Sleepless nights from a teething baby, lack of energy and a series of petty disputes on the agricultural project combine together to increase the friction out of all proportion.

Intending missionaries must be trained to spot the danger signals in a situation like this. They will need to know how to defuse the potential build-up by bringing the needs of each one concerned out into the open. Prayer and honesty and a genuine loving commitment to the good of others will show the way forward. The ability to relate to others begins with a deepening knowledge of one's own self and one's own needs. If we want to understand how people tick and how they feel, we must begin by studying ourselves in depth. We often play games with ourselves, however, pretending to be different from what we actually are, hiding the real 'me' from ourselves. Until we learn to accept this self, love it and appreciate it with its strengths and weaknesses, we cannot move forward in relating to others.

This is why missionary training institutions should make adequate space in their course for pastoral care and counselling instruction, and in our churches and fellowships we should emphasise interpersonal relationships. Do you have a group of friends with whom you can be utterly honest and who will be completely open with you? Are you learning to relate in depth to others, to identify with their situation and to minister to them in prayer and encouragement? Ask the Holy Spirit to teach you more about the shared life of Jesus as he binds his followers together to form his body.

Gaining experience: Within your local church there will be many areas where you can grow in experience and maturity. I often say to young people who are enquiring about missionary work, 'Getting on a plane won't make you a missionary. Are you a missionary at heart already? What are you doing right now to serve the Lord?'

Begin by doing a job that you feel you could enjoy — once you have conquered your nerves! If you like relating to children, volunteer to teach in the Sunday School for a couple of years. Or if older ones are more your scene, help with the teenagers. Perhaps you play the guitar, and so could offer to sing in a nearby old people's home on a Sunday afternoon.

Whatever your talent is, work hard at improving it. Take opportunities to do a day's workshop on drama or music or whatever your special interest is. Buy some books on how to improve your Sunday School teaching, or on the problems teenagers face, if they are the ones you are working with. Find out who are the experts in your particular line and take the trouble to learn from them. While at university I helped at a beach mission under the man thought to be one of the best children's workers in the country. Watching him in action and listening to him taught me a great deal.

As you go on, try to gain as wide a variety of experience as possible. When you have tackled the jobs you thought you would be good at, try some of the other ones as well. You never know what will be expected of you once you get overseas. The national church leaders are not going to tailor your job-description to suit your own personal tastes. My husband, who had been through public school and Oxford, felt that working with delinquent boys in an Approved

School would be valuable experience, and he certainly learnt some unusual things!

Cross-cultural experience: If you feel the Lord might be calling you to work among people of another nationality, try to get some initial cross-cultural experience. If there are people from that particular nation living in your own country that could be a great help. I was talking to a girl the other day who came from a large city in Britain where many Pakistanis have settled. Getting to know the ones who lived nearby so impressed her with their needs that she changed her teaching job in a school to teaching in a centre where Pakistani women can learn English. Visiting their homes and sharing their special occasions has brought her very close to them and given her insights into how they feel. If she is going to bring the love of Christ to them, the friendships she is forming are an important first step.

Have you discovered what other races live within range of your home or college? The world has been profoundly shaken in the last decades. Refugees from many nationalities have moved from one country to another. Vietnamese and Cambodians are found in many Western countries. Guest workers from Turkey flock into Germany. Immigrants from North Africa can be found in large numbers in France. When we visited Los Angeles we were told that there were more tribes people from North Thailand in the environs of that city than had remained back in Thailand!

These people are often initially lonely and bewildered. It takes them months, even years, to find their feet and put down roots. Much can be done to ease this adjustment, and in the process you will be learning valuable lessons on how to relate to people from another culture.

There may already be well-established groups from other countries near you. In most major western cities you will find a multitude of different ethnic churches. For example, in many places Chinese churches have mushroomed with locally born Chinese, overseas students, restaurant workers and others. If you are wondering about working with Chinese people you would be warmly welcomed in these fellowships. Go along to their meetings, not primarily to give, but to learn. Don't try to change things. Instead, soak in the atmosphere. Try to understand why they run things as they do and to appreciate all you see.

There are often little oases of other cultures like this right here in our Western lands, providing invaluable opportunities to begin your cross-cultural communication. As we saw in chapter 4 there are many opportunities for short-term cross-cultural experience. You could apply for summer vacation activities or one or two year terms of service with a variety of groups like IFES, OM and YWAM. Various missionary societies also offer excellent possibilities of gaining experience in another country. In this way you will be exposed to the realities of cultural adjustment and the frustrations of coping with another language. Many of our students at All Nations Christian College have already served short-term in this way. We have observed how enriching this has been for them. And they then see the relevance of what they are studying now at a missionary training college.

Structured study

A few years ago I was helping on one of the exhibition stands at Spring Harvest — a festival of praise, worship and teaching held each Easter in various centres in Britain and attended by thousands of people of all ages. Opposite me an able linguist was demonstrating how he could begin to communicate with someone whose language he did not know, and how he might identify some basic words and phrases. Over on my right an older couple were working through a computer quiz designed to test their knowledge of missionary work in the New Testament. Across the hall stood an imitation shack such as might be seen in a shanty town of South America. Here youngsters had the opportunity to spend the night in order to sample for themselves what physical deprivation might feel like.

An attractive young girl came up to me and said, 'I'm still at school but I've been thinking a lot about our responsibilities as Christians. I'm wondering if God wants me to work for him overseas somewhere, but I'm not sure how to go about it.'

'That's tremendous,' I replied, 'and it's great to be planning well ahead. Let's find somewhere to sit so we can talk a bit further.'

I led the way to a quieter part of the exhibition hall and we settled down in two easy chairs.

'Tell me first what your name is.'

'Jane,' she replied, 'Jane Stewart.'

'Well, Jane,' I continued, 'the first thing you will need to sort out is a course of further study and a career.'

Seeing a questioning look on her face I went on: 'Some countries won't let you in at all without a qualification, in dentistry, perhaps, or nutrition or teaching. And in many places where the national church is strong they have their own emerging leadership, so we need to be highly trained if we are to stand alongside them.'

'But it sounds as though it will be years and years before I can do anything positive,' she chipped in.

I laughed, 'It's not as bad as that. There'll be lots of ways in which you can serve the Lord while you're preparing. But have you ever stopped to think that if God has given you a brain and particular skills, he wants you to develop them to the full?'

We were both looking at a large poster of some African children herding their hump-backed cows. 'Lots of people in the world don't have the chance to develop their potential to the full,' I went on. 'I feel it's good stewardship of the gifts God has given us to get as good a training as possible, so that we have far more to offer to him for his use.'

'So what do you feel I should be doing in the next few years?' Jane queried, settling back more comfortably in her chair. 'How long a process will all this be?'

'Some people want to leave school as soon as possible, and "get on with life", as they see it. It's certainly great to be earning some money for the first time. But you need to be thinking about the future. If you can get into a job which trains you at the same time, that's the best to aim for. Take banking, for instance. You are learning all the time as you gain experience. There's a set course of study to follow and a series of exams to work through.

'A knowledge of banking could also be very useful in a missionary society,' I added 'They have to deal with many different currencies and constantly have to keep up to date with world-wide financial issues. For instance, when the American dollar was going through a shaky time, the Overseas Missionary Fellowship kept their money in Thai *baht* for some months, as this was the most stable currency.'

'I never thought of banking being a useful skill for a missionary!' Jane exclaimed. 'But actually, I'm about to take my A levels. I think I want to take up nursing and you can only get into the better hospitals if you have A levels. Though I might do teaching, as I do enjoy being with children . . .'

'Whatever career you take up you need to complete all the qualifications for it. For instance, if you're teaching you must do a probationary year before you are fully recognised. Really, it's wise to work in your career for at least two or three years before you think of moving on. Then you can consolidate all that you have learnt in your course until it really becomes part of you. If you choose nursing instead, you should also enquire about further training; many countries would like you to be a qualified midwife as well. Or with your interest in children you could do further paediatric training.'

'Goodness, I'll be quite antique by then!' she gasped. 'Three years for general nurse's training — that will take me from 18 to 21. Then 18 months for midwifery, at least six months for children's nursing — I'll be 23 by then!'

'That's not really antique, you know!' I laughingly replied, 'though it may feel that way to you now. Actually, the average age for people at our missionary training college is about 28-30. A lot of them have had some years overseas as well to gain cross-cultural experience first. You can do a valuable job as a short-term worker and begin to get the feel of some of the opportunities — and problems. Your missionary training will be much more meaningful if you've already had a glimpse of what it's going to be like.'

'I can't bear the thought of going to Bible college,' Jane groaned. 'If I'm going to be a missionary, I suppose I've got to go. But it sounds so holy and pious, there's no way I could fit in!'

'We're not a bunch of super-saints, by any means! And we have lots of fun, too. You should have seen us the other week when the students barricaded us into the staff room for a joke. Or when they made the Principal speak with a tasseled prayer shawl round his shoulders for his opening lecture on Judaism. Missionaries are just ordinary people, you know, and it doesn't do them any good to be set on a pedestal.

'Seriously, though, you'll find a Bible college training a fantastic privilege. Just think how great it would be to have two or three years to get to know your Bible really well, and to learn the basics of your Christian faith so that you can explain it to others. And there are so many lessons to be learnt from church history; people make the same mistakes over and over again, and if only they knew a little history they would know how to avoid them. The pastoral studies too are a tremendous help if you want to learn how to stand alongside people who are really going through it . . .'

A burst of laughter from the main hall interrupted us where the linguist was still valiantly trying to decipher the difficult language.

'But what about the missionary side? How do they train you for that?' she asked. 'I suppose you have to start by learning a foreign language?'

'Language learning comes far down the list,' I replied, 'and is not usually attempted until you get out to your new country, where you will hear it spoken all around you. It's much easier to learn a language when you are immersed in it . . . You can, of course, get training in linguistic skills before you go, which can speed up the language learning considerably.

'No, what you need to tackle first is learning about other religions and other cultures. A basic grasp of each of the world's major religions is essential. Even if you are going to a country which predominantly follows one religion, there could well be people from other groups living and working there, too. So you should have a good look at them all. Then you should study the main religion of the country in which you will be working to a far greater depth. You need to find out how their views on major issues differ from the Christian viewpoint, and how we can explain the Christian faith in terms which they will understand. There may be natural bridges between the two religions which you can make use of. And there will be many misconceptions which you need to understand and learn how to overcome.

'What do you mean?' Jane asked.

'Take the ordinary Muslim, for example. He will probably believe that the Christian doctrine of the Trinity teaches that God took a wife (Mary) who gave birth to a son (Jesus). No wonder they call that blasphemy and refuse to look any further into the Christian faith!'

'But that's crazy!' Jane expostulated, sitting bolt upright in her chair. 'We don't believe that at all!'

'I know. But you try explaining what you do believe to a Muslim! What do you mean by saying God is three persons and yet he is one? How can that be possible? And how can you say about God that there are things which he *cannot* do, when you also say he is all-powerful? The Muslims say we contradict ourselves. No wonder they dismiss the Christian doctrines!'

'Yes, it does get a bit complicated,' she agreed, sighing. 'There must be an awful lot to learn.'

'That's just the beginning of some of the things we tackle in a missionary course. There's all sorts of other things, too. Does the New Testament give us principles for missionary strategy? What can we learn from studying the history of world-wide mission and the lives of some of the great pioneers of bygone days? What problems are the younger, emerging churches facing, and how can they be nurtured into independence? What is the relationship between a spiritual ministry to other peoples and badly needed social action?'

I glanced at the look of concentration on her face and said, 'I don't want to baffle you — just whet your appetite! So that you'll see how much is involved in preparation.

'But of course one of the most important aspects is developing your own personal relationship with God. All Bible colleges put a major emphasis on this. We give high priority to the spiritual disciplines of prayer, Bible study and worship, both individual and corporate. We take time to learn how to be still in God's presence and listen to him and how to feed on his word, allowing it to prune our lives and correct our attitudes and form our basis for praise and worship.

'And it's so encouraging how students are learning to trust the Lord. Many find how wonderfully he helps them with their fees. Others have seen answers to prayer as parents' attitudes have changed towards their going overseas, or members of their family have come to know the Lord. It's important to know for yourself that God can be utterly trusted before you fly off to some remote part of the earth.'

Jane suddenly looked at her watch. 'Goodness, how time has flown!' she exclaimed. 'I'm supposed to be meeting someone, so I must go. But you've certainly given me a lot to think about.'

'Here, take some of the leaflets from the different Bible colleges,' I said as we both got to our feet. 'They'll tell you a lot more about the training offered and what experience you should have before going there.'

I picked out a sample of leaflets and handed them to her. 'Don't forget, God has a wonderful plan for your life, and he's longing to show it to you step by step. Keep your vision of missionary work really bright. It's so easy for it to grow dim in the years of preparation which are still ahead. But God will show you what to do if you keep close to him.'

Choosing a Bible college: The leaflets I handed to Jane gave information on various Bible colleges (a list of these may be obtained by writing to the Evangelical Missionary Alliance.) Each college has its own particular flavour with its own individual emphasis. It is a good idea to write to two or three different ones, requesting each to send a syllabus, and then to study these carefully. There will be various issues it would be wise to look out for: Is a good grounding in biblical knowledge provided? Is there a combination of practical spirituality with biblical and theological teaching? Is adequate emphasis placed on interpersonal relationships, growth in self-awareness and community living? Are the staff closely interacting with the students and available for group discussions and individual guidance? How much emphasis is placed on cross-cultural communication?

The calibre of the staff makes an important difference to a college. The prospective student might want to ask how many of the staff have had overseas experience. It might also be helpful to know whether the teaching is mainly done in large lectures, or in smaller seminars where exchange of views is encouraged. Some colleges run a tutorial system where each student is personally supervised and so has the opportunity of in-depth individual counsel.

It could also be useful to find out how much opportunity is given to turn academic study to practical use. Are the students helped to communicate their faith to others? What practical assignments are they given during their training?

Important, too, is the amount of time given to understanding other religions and other people's cultures and to learning the practical skills involved in communicating cross-culturally.

It is always very helpful to visit two or three colleges oneself to get the feel of them. It would not be necessary to have an interview with a member of staff unless one had already chosen to apply there. After all, the staff may be biased — indeed, they possibly should be, although their main aim will always be to help potential students find the right college, so they may recommend a different one. But the students will give their candid opinion; they know 'whether the shoe fits or where it pinches'.

When married couples are considering Bible training they should enquire what provision is made for training the wives, and whether there is a nursery for the children. In missionary work it is essential that husband and wife work as a team. The wife will be subjected to just as many pressures as her husband so they both need to be equally prepared. As we have noted before, in many countries a husband will not be able to relate personally to the women so this ministry will be the wife's responsibility. And she has her own unique gifts which should be used to the full in God's service.

On-going training: What I did not share with Jane was the whole question of on-going training. When I went to Bible college I had fondly imagined that it would give me a complete training, and I would come out the other end as the finished product. Only too soon did I discover that this was far from the case! In all walks of life people have come to see the value of on-the-job training. There is a limit to how much preparation can be given in advance. It is only after a deeper acquaintance with the situation that additional help can be offered. I have now come to realise that the initial period of training provides a foundation of knowledge and character formation and sets the prospective worker on the right course of thought and action, with the knowledge of the right questions to ask.

Many missionary societies are waking up to the need of their workers for further training and are partially providing for this in their annual conferences for members. Also, during the period of home leave it is recommended that personnel go on a refresher course. Here they can meet people from other societies and other parts of the world, share their own situation, learn from others and give and receive encouragement. At the same time teaching will be given on key issues facing missionaries today, and pastoral advice and counselling will be provided.

There is a wide variety of specialised courses which missionaries on furlough might consider taking. They could sharpen their skills in communication by further study in radio, television and video work, and in writing. Many today have felt the need for developing their skills in pastoral care and counselling which are vitally essential in mission. Further studies in anthropology or linguistics would be helpful in some situations, or a more in-depth study of the religion of the people with whom they are working. Some institutes offer specialised courses on Islamics and Judaism for those already involved in the work. Many medical workers and other experts will want to receive further training in their own field.

This whole process of training sounds long and involved, and the young person stepping gingerly onto the first rung of the ladder could feel a little daunted. But remember, training does not precede serving the Lord; the two happen simultaneously. The two should always go hand in hand and continue all our lives.

After training, what next?
During the years at Bible college students will be praying to know the Lord's will concerning the future. Are they to go overseas short term or long term? Should they serve with a

missionary society or in independent tentmaking? If it is to be with a missionary society, which one should they apply to?

If we feel it is the Lord's will that we go overseas in a professional capacity, obviously we will have to obtain a job overseas and the necessary visa. We should find out as much as possible about the country and (as we have discussed already) it could be helpful to link up, officially or unofficially, with a missionary society working there.

If we wish to serve with a missionary society, either short term or long term, some of the points mentioned in Chapter Three on choosing a society might help. It is good to form links with the society of our choice well before our college course is ended. We shall need time to visit its headquarters and meet its staff to discuss with them whether they can find a place for us in their work, and can see us fitting into their team. Attending its conferences will give us a feel of how the society functions. Taking its magazine and praying specifically for one or two of its members will help to involve us in its work.

Some people, who are not yet sure where they would fit in best, send off a copy of their *curriculum vitae* to two or three different societies. They ask the leaders to let them know whether they could see a place for them in their work. This can be a useful way of finding out where the openings lie. If we are attending a college where tutors have overseas experience or close links with missions, they will be able to advise us. It is part of the job of the college staff to know their students' personalities and gifts well enough to be able to guide them in their choice of mission and type of ministry.

When finally we become confident of the Lord's directing towards a particular missionary society, we should write to its headquarters for application papers. The whole process of applying usually takes several months. Most societies need to consult their directors overseas about their particular needs and whether we would be a suitable addition to their team. They will also require references from the pastor of

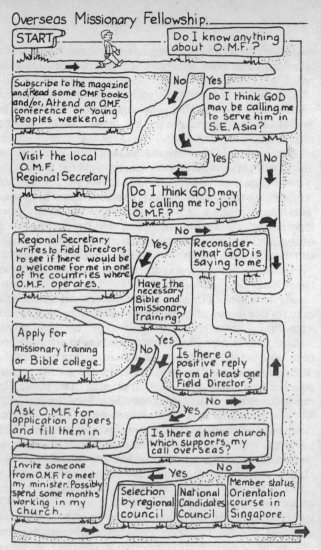

Overseas Missionary Fellowship.

START — Do I know anything about O.M.F.?

No → Subscribe to the magazine and Read some OMF books and/or, Attend an O.M.F. conference or Young Peoples weekend. → Visit the local O.M.F. Regional Secretary

Yes → Do I think GOD may be calling me to serve him in S.E. Asia?

Do I think GOD may be calling me to join O.M.F.?

Yes → Regional Secretary writes to Field Directors to see if there would be a welcome for me in one of the countries where O.M.F. operates.

No → Reconsider what GOD is saying to me.

Have I the necessary Bible and missionary training?

No → Apply for missionary training or Bible college.

Yes → Is there a positive reply from at least one Field Director?

No →

Yes → Ask O.M.F. for application papers and fill them in → Is there a home church which supports my call overseas?

Yes → Invite someone from O.M.F. to meet my minister. Possibly spend some months working in my church.

No →

Selection by regional council | National Candidates Council | Member status Orientation course in Singapore.

Example of application process when applying to a
missionary society

our church, our Bible college principal and other mature Christians about our suitability for overseas work. They will want us to have a medical certificate of fitness and to fill in doctrinal forms stating our views on various important doctrines. They may give us a language aptitude test. They will also require us to come for an interview so they can meet us personally.

The selection interview often takes the form of several days' stay at the society's headquarters, so that there is time for more leisurely talk. It is helpful for the panel of selectors to meet candidates in a more informal way than can be achieved during an ordinary interview. So there will be opportunities of worshipping together and relaxing as well as the more detailed questioning. Some selectors prefer to invite potential candidates to stay in their home for a weekend, so that they get to know them in a more natural situation.

We need not be afraid that having expressed an interest in a particular missionary society we shall then be dragooned into joining them against our will. The last thing mission leaders want is to send out new workers who are going to fit like square pegs into round holes, feeling unhappy in themselves, and spreading discontent among other missionaries. Throughout the whole application procedure their main aim will be to help us discern God's will for our life. It may be within their ranks. It may not be. They have been asked to sit on the selection panel because of their knowledge of the work overseas, their practical wisdom and maturity accumulated over the years, and their close walk with God. In meeting them and discussing our future with them, we shall have the privilege of making use of these gifts to help us discern God's way for our life.

If the selection panel does not feel we should be joining their society this should not be regarded in any way as a 'rejection', but as a redirection. God has his perfect plans for each one of us, and he wants us to walk his chosen path with joy and confidence.

If we are accepted for service the leaders will discuss with us how soon we can be ready to go. Some find themselves leaving within a few weeks or months, others may need longer to settle affairs at home, strengthen their links with their church, or gain further experience. Each candidate will be treated as an individual, taking into account his or her own particular circumstances. All the preparation will now be drawing towards its goal.

Questions for discussion
1. What professional and personal training have you had already? What has God taught you through it?
2. What would you expect to gain from Bible college and missionary training?
3. Have you ever related to people of another race? What did you learn about their culture and your own?

7

Who will support me?

The importance of a home church

In our chapter on the biblical basis of mission we saw the important role which their home church played in the missionary career of Paul and Barnabas. They were already recognised leaders in the church in Antioch of Syria, and played their part as prophets and teachers. One day, as all the leaders were worshipping and fasting together, the Holy Spirit instructed them to set Barnabas and Paul apart for the task of missionary work (Acts 13:1,2). So the leaders laid hands on the two men, sending them off to preach the Gospel in other lands.

We cannot imagine that from then on the Christians in Antioch washed their hands of Paul and Barnabas, and disclaimed all further responsibility for them. These New Testament churches consisted of people who loved and cared for each other. In the first flush of joy in their Christian life some new believers had pooled all their resources, selling everything they had and using it for the common good (Acts 4:32–35). This probably did not take place everywhere, but it was indicative of the tremendous warmth and love which was to be found in those early groups of Christians.

We can picture the church in Antioch praying fervently for their two representatives as they left, asking for success on their mission and safety in travel. We can imagine them passing round every scrap of news which came from the two travellers via others who had met them, or through letters. And the joyful reception which welcomed them back when they returned would have left Paul and Barnabas in no doubt that, although they had been away for years, the church in Antioch still considered them a part of their fellowship (Acts 14:26–28).

We all need to belong to a church. The New Testament writers had no concept of solitary Christians. And the pattern they show us is that missionaries are to be called out from churches to go and found other churches.

In the last decades of the twentieth century there has been much to discourage us from following the biblical ideal. Populations are no longer static. Employment and education needs force a greater mobility onto our society, so that many people today are not members of a specific church. But whether or not we are called to missionary work, we need to ask God which church we should join, and then give it our full commitment and support. We should offer to shoulder responsibility within the fellowship, reaching out in love and friendship to others. All of us should do all we can to build up this branch of the church of Christ in which God has set us *now*.

Perhaps it will be the leaders of our church who will approach us and say, 'We feel God is calling you into a special work for him. Have you ever considered missionary work overseas?' In such a case we will have the confirmation that it is not only our own inclination which is driving us forward, but others have had a prompting from the Holy Spirit along the same lines.

Perhaps our church is not very mission-minded and has never had anything to do with missionary societies, let alone sent out their own missionary. This could be a God-given opportunity for us gently and lovingly to widen their horizons. We can start by passing a missionary magazine around for others to look at, or share some missionary biographies with our friends. If we are members of a home group we might be able to ask prayer for a friend of ours who is working overseas; regular reports on their situation will help promote an interest in their work. Our minister might be willing to have a missionary to speak from time to time, and this could lead on to regular missionary weekends when the whole church is thinking about overseas mission. We should not be worried about starting small; many worthwhile projects have small beginnings. But we do need patience, gentleness and stickability in order to nurture a missionary interest where none existed before.

It is particularly important that our church leaders should have a worldwide vision themselves and encourage this in their congregations. It could be most helpful to encourage the minister or elders to visit mission situations abroad, and thus see for themselves the needs and opportunities. If the leadership team are aflame with the fever of missionary vision they will ensure that their members catch it also. They will notice the biblical emphasis on 'the nations', 'the Gentiles' and 'the world', and consistently bring this international aspect into their teaching and preaching. And they will want to make sure that there is an active missionary committee in the church which will stimulate prayerful support for their missionaries and encourage others to serve overseas. 'Love your local missionary' edited by Martin Goldsmith provides practical hints for this.

Everyone going overseas needs the backing of a home church. And the time before going out provides a valuable opportunity for strengthening our links with our home base. Some churches like a missionary candidate to work with them for a period of time before leaving, so that everyone really gets to know them well. Here is a chance to serve others and minister to their needs. The measure we give to others will be the measure we receive, both now and in the future (Luke 6:38).

Some people talk a great deal about financial support for missionaries. Actually, it is not so much support we should be looking for as a relationship of love. We need to aim at the New Testament model of genuine love. 'Make love your aim,' Paul wrote to the Corinthian Christians (I Corinthians 14:1). If someone is loved, of course their physical needs will be taken care of, of course they will be prayed for, encouraged and helped in every way possible. So we must pray for deepening love within our fellowship. Love is a two-way movement. One party should not be doing all the giving and the other all the receiving. As we receive from our church fellowship we shall want to give back to them — in service before we go, in praying while we are overseas, in letter-writing and caring.

Right from the earliest days of our interest in mission it is good for our church fellowship to know about it. Praying with the leaders before we take each successive step will help to clarify our guidance, and also to make everyone feel we are all in it together. If some people are not happy with our moving into full-time Christian work, it is much better if they express their opinion early on. Then we can seek the Lord's mind together, and a corporate decision may be arrived at.

If we belong to a loving and spiritually open church, its members can be of tremendous help in advising us along the way, encouraging us when the preparation appears long and tedious or when difficulties threaten to block our path. Their expertise could help us decide which part of the world to work in and which missionary society to apply to. But we must remember to have patience with our spiritual leaders. The perfect church has not yet been set up on earth. As someone once remarked, 'If the perfect church does exist, don't join it. You'd be bound to spoil it!' So if we sometimes want to echo the caption on the poster which says, 'Have patience with me, God hasn't finished with me yet', it is as well to remember that the same applies to our church leaders. They may not yet be giving us all the support we long for, but they too are on the path of learning.

If there is a relationship of love between us and the church, both sides will want to maintain strong ties as we move overseas. Those much-dreaded prayer letters which we are expected to write can actually become the means of keeping friendship strong. They can be a joy, rather than a duty or drudgery, if approached in the right way. Cassettes make communication so much easier nowadays. To be able to listen in to our home church worshipping together or to a teaching session, can be like water in an arid desert. And they will enjoy the wide variety of new sounds which we can capture on tape and our description of life overseas.

The value of prayer
One of the main reasons for writing and sending cassettes will be to help our friends back at home pray for us. Praying is not an easy task. Many may ask enthusiastically for our letters before we leave, but the numbers of those who will persevere continuously for the three or four years before we return will probably be few. Yet prayer is one of the most important tools we have to accomplish God's work. When Paul described in such detail the evil forces arrayed against us, he enumerated the spiritual weapons God has given us to combat them. The final item on his list is prayer, which he describes in great detail, as if to underline its importance. 'Pray in the Spirit on *all* occasions with *all* kinds of prayers and requests', (that is, anywhere and everywhere use every kind of prayer we know). 'With this in mind, be alert and *always keep on praying* for *all* the saints' (Ephesians 6:18). Paul could hardly have used stronger words! He was emphatic that as we go out to storm the kingdom of darkness

our ultimate weapon is prayer. It is primarily prayer which changes things.

Here we see the beauty of God's economy. Not everyone is called to go overseas, although sometimes the impression is given that those who stay behind are second-class citizens! Many who for one reason or another are not able to go, somehow feel themselves to be inferior. But this is not at all the correct picture. As the support group prays, they *are part of the action*. They are just as much involved in it as those who are 'on the job'. We see this clearly in the story of Aaron and Hur steadying Moses' hands as he prayed for the Israelites fighting the Amalekites (Exodus 17: 8–13). In point of fact, those who prayed had a *more* important role to play than those who fought (though neither was effective without the other). And it was the continual, persistent, unwavering prayer which made all the difference.

As we live and work overseas, our part in the exercise will be to inform those at home of such facts, descriptions and incidents as will make them want to pray for us. We should find out all we can about the country where we are working — its geography, history, political situation etc., and then carefully break this up into interesting morsels to feed back home. An overview of the situation, not just the tiny angle or perspective which our own work gives, is often interesting, and we can help our prayer partners to get the feel of the situation by giving some descriptions as well as facts.

Before we set out it is good to establish a missionary prayer group. If we are the first missionaries to go out from our church this group will probably be focussing on our work. But the aim could be to expand it to care for other people or types of work overseas as well. I know one group where they divide up into twos or threes, each praying for a different part of the world, and when they meet together they can each share what they have learnt.

Our goal should be for the whole church to be praying. To this end it is helpful if the missionaries' names are mentioned and prayed for in the main services. This will remind everyone that we are still part of the body of Christ in that locality, and that the whole church should be behind us in prayer and support.

A Sunday school teacher I know, who has prayed faithfully for a missionary couple for many years, always talks about them to her class. Each week she tells about one aspect of their work, and then the children pray for them. It

four minutes a time, but over the year
s the children develop a deep interest in
concern for their work. It would be
h classes were doing the same with other
t during their years in Sunday school the
a fair knowledge of missionary work of

ur prayer needs we must not forget to
s to prayer which have come. If we look
letters we can share with our friends at
raying has made all the difference. There
t of encouragement to aid perseverance!
porting church we shall probably have
red through all the places we have lived
d. Martin and I found that many of our
e days supported us faithfully over the
hey did not belong to a group which met
also be given the names of some people
porters of our missionary society or of
ur part of the world. We may find it
hese folks whom we have never met, and

a p   om them will be a help, plus a description of their family and work. For us it became much easier to relate more deeply to these people once we made a point of meeting them on our next home leave.

Financial matters

Someone was once asked, 'What do you think of when you hear the word "missionary"?' And the answer came back, 'Someone asking for money.'

What an unfortunate description! But it can be uncomfortably true. This is why I have kept financial matters towards the end of the book, so that they may not dominate unduly.

When talking about his deputation programme, visiting churches and telling them about what God was doing for China, Hudson Taylor said, 'I always aim to go to a church in order to give. If you are wondering all the time how much money this meeting will raise, you can't listen for what God wants to tell them through you. God will take care of the money.' On another occasion he remarked, 'I notice it is not difficult for me to remember that my own children need breakfast in the morning, dinner at midday and something before they go to bed at night. Indeed, I could not forget it. And I find it impossible to suppose that our Heavenly Father is less tender or mindful than I.'

We have been called to the high privilege of serving the living God who made heaven and earth. He will not fail or leave us in the lurch. He always cares for his own. God has promised to meet all our needs (Philippians 4:19). However, we have to realise that what we need and what we *want* are not necessarily the same thing. God may see fit to allow us to live overseas far more simply than we have been used to at home. There may be times of war, drought or famine when even the most basic items are difficult to come by. I passed some years of my childhood held as a prisoner by the Japanese because my parents were missionaries in China. The camp of 1,400 people was desperately overcrowded, short of food and lacking the necessary fuel to keep us warm against the bitter cold of the north China winters. And yet I can say that even in those conditions God supplied all our needs.

The comparative comfort and luxury of life in the West has spoilt us. Here at home we take for granted a high standard of living, and gradually add all the newest amenities and gadgets. So many of us have shut our eyes to the conditions in which two thirds of the world live, and we have forgotten the dedication and self-sacrifice of missionaries in earlier times. In the days of pioneer evangelism, missionaries were prepared to trek on foot for days over wild countryside, to sleep on a mud floor, to live in a house with no running water and certainly no electricity, and to eat whatever food grew locally. Their enthusiasm to take the Gospel to every place where Christ was unknown was not to be dampened by physical difficulties.

Times have changed. The church has been established in many remote parts. Urbanisation has swept millions of people from the countryside into the cities. So how are we to decide at what standard we should be living and therefore how much finance we shall need for our support? Some missionaries in countries where inflation is rampant or living is expensive will need more money for their support, some will need less. Those who are 'tent-makers' will hardly need any at all, since they are supporting themselves. Some forms of mission are more expensive, such as those necessitating the purchasing and upkeep of expensive equipment. For instance, the Missionary Aviation Fellowship keeps a fleet of light planes in action, and this requires large sums of money. Other societies maintain expensive radio broadcasting systems.

Each missionary's expenditure depends upon the appropriate standard of living for their situation. To decide on an appropriate standard of living overseas we need to consider who are the people we are hoping to reach in the new environment. It is their standard of living which we should make our own. It may be much simpler than we have been used to, but the spiritual principle of identification should help us take on this new level of living with joy. Some missionaries may find themselves working in wealthy cities, with very comfortable homes and every convenience. It is almost more difficult to find the right balance here. We should not be extravagant with money which has been sacrificially given by God's people, and yet our home needs to be of sufficient standard for the local people to feel at ease visiting us.

Mission leaders can offer helpful advice on choosing a right balance, but missionaries need to recognise that standards of living will vary from place to place. We may be tempted to feel discontented if others in our mission are living more comfortably than we are. Yet the task of mission inevitably calls for sacrifice.

Comparison between living standards of workers from different missions can also promote jealousy. I remember visiting a desert area where the people were nomads, and the only shelter they built for themselves was a small primitive awning of grass, open on one side and storing a few cooking utensils. The American missionaries had built themselves a two-storey solid breeze-block house. They had their own generator to pump water and provide power for lighting, refrigerator and a deep-freeze. The baby's battery-driven toys, clipped onto the side of her play-pen, seemed the most incongruous objects I had ever seen! In contrast the European missionaries working in the same area had built themselves a very much smaller, simpler home. During our brief visit I wondered what the feelings between the two families were. As Martin and I discussed it afterwards we agreed it was extremely difficult to know where to pitch one's standard of living in a situation like this. It would be almost impossible for a missionary family to live like the local people, though there was a single man who was doing so. The temptation for jealousy and criticism to grow between the two families would be great unless they were on their guard against it.

Raising support: Different missionary societies have been led to different methods for raising their support. As we consider applying to a society, we must make sure we feel comfortable with its way of handling its finance. Some systems suit one person better than another, the choice often being determined by temperament, upbringing and our general way of looking at things. Let us not criticise others for the way they feel God has led them. Let us rather be free to choose for ourselves what we feel to be right for us.

Some denominational societies fix a set salary for their workers, and this commits them to raising a specific sum of money. If they have the backing of large churches this may not be too difficult, but in these days of inflation and growing costs it requires a good deal of faith to raise this money. New workers may only be accepted when there is enough finance in hand to pay for them. The setting up of new projects is limited in the same way.

Other societies feel that this method would unduly restrict the numbers of new workers they accept, and so organise themselves differently. Every new worker is asked to raise their own support before going out. The missionary candidate is expected to approach their home church and other Christian friends and tell them frankly how much it will cost to send them overseas and maintain them there. If a church fully acknowledges its own responsibility it may respond by saying, 'You are a member of our community. We feel you belong to us just as much when you are overseas as when you are at home. We should like to take full responsibility for all your needs, and we shall budget accordingly.' Many churches, for one reason or another, cannot go as far as this and so undertake to cover a certain proportion of the expenses. Other Christian friends may then make up the difference, and when the stated amount per year is finally promised the new worker is free to go overseas.

This system allows for tremendous flexibility, as more and more workers can be added without straining central funds. Some of the largest missions, and the ones which have seen the most rapid growth in personnel, work this way. A fixed percentage of the gifts given to a particular person is required to be handed over for central administrative purposes.

Then, too, there are societies which pool their funds. Any money given to an individual missionary or to the society itself goes into a central fund from which all expenses are paid. All missionaries receive the same amount of money, from the General Director down to the newest workers: whatever comes in is shared among them, in proportion to the cost of living in their area. Thus, some months much money may be distributed and other months very little at all. Those who practise this method feel that it emphasises the equal value of all their workers. Under the own-support system, those who are gifted speakers or who are able to go out and do eye-catching work may find it comparatively easy to raise support, whereas others, who are not doing such spectacular jobs, may find their money coming in more slowly. But the system of pooling money means that all workers in all situations receive the same amount and are not judged by their gifts or work situation.

The reasons for the different systems are largely to be found in the early history of the particular societies and in the character of the sending countries. In America, which is noted for its generous concern for individuals and warmth of personal relationships, missionary giving is usually done by personal support of individuals. The older societies in Europe expected all money to be placed in the central fund, and the workers were either paid a fixed salary or the money was divided up as it came in. Some of the newer societies and those who have revised their system follow the more personalised method of raising support.

In some countries the pattern of giving will be affected by taxation laws. If these give tax relief to charities it can be more advantageous to give to the central funds of the missionary society rather than directly to the individual. The value of any one contribution may be increased enormously because of this. As Christians we have a responsibility to give wisely as well as generously.

Other forms of support: If there is a genuine relationship of love between the home church and the outgoing missionary, support will consist of far more than merely praying and promising to give a certain amount of money. Real concern should stimulate the imagination to put oneself in the other person's shoes. Those at home will be sensitive to the feelings of disorientation and uselessness which can so easily come in the early days, and frequent cards or letters are a great encouragement during this period. To have one's birthday remembered faithfully each year can be a lovely surprise. Even small gifts can be greatly appreciated by people living in an area where Western goods are unobtainable. We remember in Sumatra celebrating one occasion with a packet of Smarties. They had never tasted so good! A copy of that newly published book which is being such a help to many in the home church could be sent out for the missionary to enjoy. A regular subscription to a Christian magazine helps the expatriate to keep up-to-date with what is going on at home. But remember when sending printed matter to make sure none of it impinges upon the national sensitivities of the overseas country.

Some of us do not find it easy to use our imagination on behalf of others, but I have found praying specifically about this to have made a big difference. When I have taken time to lift someone in prayer to God asking for his blessing, and then asking if there is anything I can do for that person, the Lord has often put a new idea into my mind.

Although the home church should always retain the invaluable position of acting as a sounding board for its missionaries, when a new worker goes overseas the immediate responsibility for them is, in a sense, handed over to their missionary society and to the national church. This is inevitable, since they are the ones on the spot who know the local situation, with all its complexities, opportunities and problems. Much unhappiness and tension can be caused when the home church attempts to retain too tight a hold on its member overseas as it is difficult fully to appreciate the intricacies of their task. Even a visit cannot disclose to home church members all the cultural differences of the new situation. But they can act very helpfully by giving advice as they see it, and by maintaining the impartiality of a relative 'outsider'.

If the new worker has received a good missionary training they may also from time to time seek advice from the staff of their college. If they have had overseas experience they will have some understanding of the problems, yet being outside the situation will provide a measure of impartiality.

Equipment

When we lived in Malaysia a family of new missionaries moved into another town, bringing with them case upon case of luggage. It transpired that they had brought all their European furniture with them, as they had possessed such a beautiful house back home. The heavy, upholstered chairs looked quite out of place in a tropical country where all furniture was cool and light to allow air to circulate. I often wondered whether the couple could bear the heat of sitting in those chairs for any length of time, in an atmosphere of such sticky humidity that perspiration trickled slowly down one's back even when sitting still! This family must have shipped their goods out with the best intentions, but they failed to appreciate in advance the vast differences in lifestyle between different countries. And they had not asked each other the more important question, 'Will the local people feel at ease with us if we set up a Western style home in their town?'

Because many of us have not even visited the country in which we shall be working, we need to take the advice of others already living there concerning the equipment we should bring. Any missionary society will be very experienced in helping with this. Or we can write to an expatriate family out there and ask their advice. Generally speaking, all the larger items are best left at home as these are the ones that will stick out most in the new country.

Smaller items can also seem fabulously wealthy in some situations. We were determined to manage without a car when we lived in North Sumatra, but I discovered to my consternation that the two bicycles we had bought in Singapore were the envy of the neighbourhood — you could not buy anything of such good quality locally. My despair mounted when even our drawing pins were commented on, because we could use them to pin a poster on our wooden walls and they would not bend! We soon realised that if we wanted to be fully accepted into the local community, the less goods we brought in from abroad the better.

Many missionaries prefer to bring in the bare minimum and purchase locally whatever they need, though most of us will have some extras which we really would appreciate. We enjoyed a radio and a record player. (Our neighbours had radios which played loudly most of the day, but we appreciated being able to listen to our own music sometimes and to hear the BBC World Service.) We had a camera, too, but we kept this quiet for a long time as no one else we knew possessed one. But the greatest difference between us and our neighbours lay in the amount of books we possessed. Fortunately, the locals were quite prepared to accept that ministers needed books for their study and sermon preparation.

Books of all sorts can be a tremendous asset. Many missionaries do not get much spiritual input while overseas, as the sermons in the local church and their teaching workshops are quite rightly geared to the needs of the local people. So it is important to be able to feed ourselves from the Bible, from commentaries and other devotional books. Exchanging these books with others will add to the variety of reading matter, and some lighter reading is a help, too. We enjoyed biographies, both Christian and secular, historical books and a variety of other forms of writing. As a missionary team we passed around some of the classic writings of spiritual depth, such as *The Life of Andrew Bonar* and *Whitefield's Journals*.

When praying about and planning what equipment to take overseas, let us not forget that our Lord gave up the glory of heaven and lived in complete identification with those

around him in order to be able to communicate his message more clearly to them. We too should be willing to do this. Our aim is to make as small as possible the feeling of foreignness which others will have towards us, by adapting as far as possible to their language, their customs and their lifestyle. Only in this way will we earn the right to draw alongside them as friends and share our wonderful message with them.

In primitive societies this can be costly, leading to a complete lack of privacy and a very poor diet. I have friends who have lived among nomads where the basic diet is milk and blood, only occasionally alleviated by some camel meat. Another friend lives in an African hamlet where all her property belongs to the community, and if she prepares food at all anyone else is free to drop in and eat it. These situations demand much wisdom, and not everyone is called to such rigorous self-sacrifice. Although Jesus calls us to deny ourselves and follow him, we should not be bringing much honour to his name if we had to be invalided home on health grounds!

On the other hand, certain types of work need more specialised, expensive equipment. Some forms of medicine, agricultural development or mass media production necessitate the spending of large amounts of money. All the time we should be asking ourselves what equipment and lifestyle is appropriate for each particular situation.

Much radical thinking has been going on as people have begun to realise that setting up highly equipped, expensive-to-run hospitals may not be the wisest solution to the health problems overseas. Community centres with specialists in primary health care might be more appropriate.

So as we plan what equipment to take and what lifestyle to adopt, let us be prepared to take advice from others and to go as learners. And let us try to share our goals with our home church, so the people there can appreciate some of the issues we are grappling with and be able to give us the support we need.

Questions for discussion
1. What are you contributing to your present church?
2. Describe your relationship to the leadership of your church.
3. What are you doing in support of a missionary?

8

Where Do I Go from Here?

Although it is now more than 30 years ago I still remember the thrill I felt when we set out for the first time for Singapore. Representatives from our home churches came to see us off. My family drove down to Southampton docks to be with us. Cards and flowers and letters had been showered on us, and we set off with a sense of excitement which fortunately outweighed our tinges of anxiety and homesickness. You may or may not have the privilege of a joyful and loving farewell, but there is no doubt that leaving to serve God overseas has a special excitement all of its own.

The time spent in another country can be tremendously enriching. When we returned on our first leave and compared notes with many of our friends, it came home to us how privileged we had been in the amazing variety of experiences we had been through during our four years away. There had been opportunities to experience God's personal love for us and his miraculous power in providing for us all along the way. We had visited exotic places and seen the beauty of God's creation in tropical rain forests, unspoiled, palm-fringed beaches, majestic volcanoes and fertile plateaus. We had made many new friends who had expanded our horizons and enriched us personally. Our understanding of our own faith had been challenged as we had begun to see Christianity through other people's eyes. Many aspects of the Bible had come alive for us in a new way through living in a community-based Asian society with its more leisurely pace and agricultural setting. Old assumptions had been challenged and new lessons appreciated, and we knew ourselves to have been deeply enriched in our own personalities.

I admit that I had gone overseas expecting to give (and with my privileged Western background it was right that I should do so), but I had gained far more than I had given in those four years. The following years of service in South East Asia confirmed to me that God is nobody's debtor. When we imagine that we are giving up everything to follow Christ, he responds with such tender love and overflowing blessings that we cannot think why we had ever considered it a 'sacrifice'.

Attitudes count

This is not to deny the difficulties. This book has already clearly portrayed some of the things which may not be easy to adjust to. But it is our attitude which matters most. If we arrive at our destination with an open mind which is prepared for many things to be different, it will be much easier for us. A teacher at the International High School in Khartoum wrote to me:

'It makes me so sad to hear all the complaining and the grumbling here. There is so much talk about the things we can't get, whereas I'm constantly grateful for the things which *are* available.'

It is her attitude which has made all the difference. The issue was: with whom would she mentally compare herself, folk back home or the desperately poor people around her? She knew that whatever our circumstances there are always people worse off than ourselves, and so was able to cultivate an attitude of thankfulness.

2 2

2 2

2 2

Culture shock

There is bound to be some measure of culture shock when moving from one society to another where our own well-tried methods and views will be challenged. After her three-month tour of the Indian subcontinent a friend vividly described to me how degraded she felt as a woman being jostled in a Bangladesh market. All her feminine hackles had risen when she saw first-hand how Muslim men regard the women in their community.

Martin remembers the feelings of indignation which welled up in him when he was accused of flirting with a woman in South Thailand. They had passed each other on their bicycles on their way to work once a week, and he had presumed to smile at her and use the one Thai phrase he knew in wishing her 'good morning'. And I know how bewildered and alone I felt during my first few days in Sumatra when Martin was away extricating our luggage from the clutches of the customs officials.

Culture shock can make people react in a variety of ways. Often small irritations which normally would not be considered important become disproportionately threatening. At the orientation centre in Singapore where we used to work, feelings once ran ludicrously high over whether we should eat our boiled eggs the American way in a bowl or the British way in an egg-cup. We laugh when we think of it now, but in an unfamiliar situation small things may provide the security we are desperately seeking. Their removal threatens us more than we could ever anticipate. A first Christmas overseas can often be a traumatic time, when cherished family traditions are replaced by unfamiliar activities. Homesickness can be fiercely painful at times like these.

Another result of culture shock may be the development of an intense dislike for certain things. The sight and smell of the stagnant monsoon drains in Jakarta so disgusted one missionary he found it extremely difficult to live there. Quite small things can make us over-react to such an extent that a growing prejudice against the country as a whole and its people develops. We noticed this the few times we mixed in expatriate circles in Sumatra. The business personnel appeared to be competing with each other as to who could relate the most telling tales against the Indonesians. There were plenty of stories to be told of inefficiency and unnecessary bureaucracy, which led to an ever-increasing volume of complaints. This, of course, soured their relationships with the local people, and if we were going to retain them as our friends there was no way we could join in such conversations.

In the early months of culture shock it is important to realise what is going on and deal with it accordingly. The striking changes we have to face and the amount of adjustment involved in coming to terms with our new situation may well threaten our personal security and identity. We must take our feelings to the Lord and pour out our heart to him. Frustrations are best vented at God and not at our fellow workers! Patience, both with ourselves and with others, is needed. We require time to adjust to each other. And we must refuse to follow the Israelites' sin of murmuring in discontent against God. Deliberately settling down to count your blessings will help, as will remembering that we can always 'rejoice in the Lord' (Philippians 4:1) when we can't see anything else in which to rejoice!

Climate: A hot, sticky climate such as we had to face in Singapore can lead to difficulties in sleep, poor concentration and irritability. With the incessant heat everything can become a tremendous effort, and we may constantly feel tired and apathetic. Relationships can be spoiled as the tension level mounts.

Here again practical common sense is needed. It helps to slow down our Western pressurised mentality to the speed of the local people. They are not going to judge us by our work output but by the attractiveness of our character. When they take a siesta we can make sure we get one too, so that our

146

activity coincides with the coolest part of the day. The day's programme can be adjusted to fit in with the sun so that, for instance, we cook our main meal in the evening, and don't have to stand over a hot stove in the midday-heat. It takes time to become acclimatised. It may take up to six months, but we should not let that worry us. We can refuse to be bullied into the rushed outlook of a Westerner.

Food: The local food may be a source of strain in a new country. When we worked among the Chinese in Singapore, food was a sheer delight, and one could not find a healthier diet anywhere. But in North Sumatra the lavish use of chillies in the food drowned every other flavour. Sometimes we could not tell whether it was fish or meat we were eating! And at Martin's first Synod meeting the food was so spicy, moisture poured from his eyes and nose until it looked as if he was crying! The other delegates teased him mercilessly about it; but he did find that the incident broke down any barriers between them when they saw he could laugh at himself. Over the years we discovered that the most unpalatable dish eventually could taste quite nice, if one kept persevering. But if we fail to eat the dishes they set before us, however unusual the flavour or simple the diet, we can cause deep offense.

Language: 'I was never any good at French at school so I'll never learn the language,' was the gloomy comment from one of the young people we met in Chapter Four. But there is a world of difference between school language lessons and language learnt in the country where it is spoken, and where we shall hear it all around us. Our motivation to grasp it becomes much stronger. We learn expressions which we can try out that very same day in local homes and in the market. And the more courage we have to 'break the sound barrier' and start using the language, the better. The Rabbinic statement 'a shy man learns nothing' is particularly true of language acquisition.

The process of language learning has been made very much easier and quicker through the modern science of linguistics. In the late 1960s an American fellow worker at the language centre in Singapore told us how at the end of her first four years of service she still had not completely sorted out the seven tones in the Hokkien language. So how could she begin to communicate?

Since then, much ground has now been covered, and a great deal of thought has been given to the most efficient methods of learning a language, so that the new missionary will find plenty of aids. Even if there are as yet no grammar books or dictionaries in the language you are studying the Wycliffe Bible Translator's Summer Institute in Linguistics course which is held in many countries will show you how to tackle this formidable task.

If we are going out with a missionary society, it is wise to ask about language study policy, and if necessary, negotiate for an adequate length of time to be given to it. To be told, for instance, that we are going to be given three months for the study of Arabic is laughable. This is a complex language and difficult to master. A whole year will give us a good start but we shall need to build considerably on that. For Japanese an initial two years solid language study is desirable, and if we are going to spend twenty or thirty years in that land, this will be time well invested.

It is worth spending time and effort on acquiring good language, otherwise we shall be ham-strung in our ministry. If we are not going overseas with a mission this may be more difficult to achieve, but it should still be our goal.

Unless inhibited by a real blockage over language learning, all new missionaries will reach a certain level of fluency where they can hold conversations and preach a simple message. Self-discipline is needed to take our study beyond that to the point where we feel really at home in the language, and the local people sense our facility is great enough for them to confide in us. Living in a local home if we are single, or opening our home to others if we are married, will help greatly here. But there are no short cuts. Language acquisition demands a high degree of motivation and continuing perseverance. Yet the rewards are great when we find the nationals chatting to us as they would to each other. A good grasp of the language will form a basis for a life-time's service towards the fulfilment of God's world-wide mission purposes.

The final goal

The last book of the Bible portrays vividly our sovereign God ruling over this entire world, controlling the course of history, and despite all opposition bringing it to his own predetermined climax. The venerable and saintly apostle John was granted the privilege of looking into heaven itself and glimpsing the reality which exists there. He describes for us the radiant throne of God surrounded by worshipping, glorious angelic beings. As John watched, the Lamb which had been slain came forward and took the scroll from the hand of him who sat on the throne. At once a burst of song went up:

> You are worthy to take the scroll
> and to open its seals,
> because you were slain,
> and with your blood you purchased men
> to God
> from every tribe and language and people and
> nation.
> You have made them to be a kingdom
> and priests to serve our God
> and they will reign on the earth.
>
> (Revelation 5:9,10)

This was the reason why Christ died — to purchase for God people from every tribe, language, people and nation. God is deeply concerned for *everyone*. There is no racial group outside his love, no tribe for which he did not send his

Son. Have we not therefore a great responsibility to make sure that everyone knows about Christ's priceless sacrifice? Is not our highest duty that of making the Gospel known to every city, every town, every remote hamlet on this earth?

The Moravians, who more than 250 years ago formed the first major missionary thrust of the modern era, took as their slogan 'Our Lamb has conquered; let us follow him.' The great motivation behind their zeal was that the Lamb might receive the due reward for his work. 'How can it be,' they asked, 'that the very Lamb of God has died, but he must keep waiting patiently for the reward which he has won because men and women are too slack to shoulder the responsibility God has given them?'

The apostle Paul demonstrates for us this same sense of urgency and commitment to the one over-riding goal. He writes; 'Christ's love compels us, because we are convinced that one died for all, and therefore all died. And he died for all, that those who live should no longer live for themselves but for him who died for them and was raised again' (II Corinthians 5:14,15). The word Paul uses for 'compel' is a word which contains the idea of 'constrain'. Paul felt the constraint of the love of Christ in his life, narrowing down his diffuse goals to one over-riding ambition. Christ's love would not allow Paul's energies to be dissipated into other, lesser tasks.

In the Cameron Highlands of Malaysia I was once taken to see the huge dam which had been built to generate hydro-electric power. All the weight of water in the high mountain lake was brought into one channel to rush down the massive pipes and provide the power to generate a vast amount of electricity. Standing there listening to the roar of water rushing past us, I saw in a new way what it means for the love of Christ to constrain us. His love in us and our love for him narrows us down to only one ambition: to make Christ known throughout the whole world. When we have truly seen Christ's love, how costly was his sacrifice and how magnificent are his plans for all mankind, then we too shall find ourselves compelled to pursue the one, all-important goal.

Mission possible
No longer may we live for ourselves, but for Christ alone. The Son of God died to procure the salvation of the world. No sacrifice is too great to make for him in our response. He offers new life to all and wants us to be his messengers. Here is the vision for a world which needs Christ. Let us keep the challenge of his call clearly in view as we progress through the necessary steps of getting there from here.

Questions for discussion
1. What aspects of missionary life could make you anxious? Has God got an answer for this?
2. How do you cope now with pressures and difficulties?
3. Do you have ambitions or desires which actually rival God for the primary place in your life?

Appendix

Missionary Societies and Bible Training Courses

Addresses of many missionary societies with UK offices, and Bible Colleges with training courses appropriate to missionary service, can be obtained from:

Evangelical Missionary Alliance
Whitefield House
186 Kennington Park Road
London SE11 4BT

Among correspondence courses available, the following are recommended:

The Open Theological College
PO Box 220
The Park Campus
The Park
Cheltenham
GL50 2QF

St John's Extension Studies
Chilwell Lane
Bramcote
Nottingham
NU9 3DS

Bibliography

Books by Martin Goldsmith

Islam and Christian Witness (OM Publishing 1987)
What about Other Faiths? (Hodder & Stoughton 1989)
What in the World is God Doing? (Monarch 1991)
Who is My Neighbour? with Rosemary Harley (Scripture Union 1992)

Other 'Next Step' Books

Cooper, Anne *Ismael, My Brother*, (Monarch 1993)
Donovan, Vincent *Christianity Rediscovered* (SCM 1978)
Elsdon, Ron *Greenhouse Theology* (Monarch 1992)
Griffiths, Michael *Get Your Church Involved in Missions* (OMF 1974)
Lion Handbook to the World's Religions, The (Lion 1994)
Riggans, Walter *Covenant with the Jews*, (Monarch 1992)
Sider, Ronald *Evangelism and Social Action* (Hodder & Stoughton 1993)
Wardell, Margaret and Robin Thomson *Entering Another's World* (St John's Extension Studies 1994)
Wright, Chris *What's So Unique about Jesus?* (Monarch 1990)